LEONTES

Whatever you can make her do, I'm
Whatever you can make her say, I'm ~~happy to hear,~~
because it must be as easy to make her speak as it is to
make her move.

PAULINA

It's necessary that you have faith. So everyone hold
still, and anyone who thinks this is bad business should
leave now.

LEONTES

Go ahead. No one will move.

PAULINA

Music, wake her!

Music plays.

It's time. Come down, and no longer be stone.
Come forward. Make everyone who looks at you
be amazed. Come, I'll fill up your grave. Move, no,
move away, let Death have your numbness since life
is taking you from **him**. You see she moves.

> *That is, from Death.*

HERMIONE *comes down.*

Don't jump. Her actions are pure, and this spell is no evil
enchantment. Don't shun her, because if you do, you'll
kill her all over again. No, put your hand forward. You
courted her when she was young. Now in old age does she
have to court you?

LEONTES

Oh, she's warm! If this is magic, it should be as ordinary
as eating.

POLIXENES

She embraces him.

CAMILLO

> She hangs about his neck:
> If she pertain to life let her speak too.

POLIXENES

> Ay, and make it manifest where she has lived,
> Or how stolen from the dead.

PAULINA

140
> That she is living,
> Were it but told you, should be hooted at
> Like an old tale: but it appears she lives,
> Though yet she speak not. Mark a little while.
> Please you to interpose, fair madam: kneel
145
> And pray your mother's blessing. Turn, good lady;
> Our Perdita is found.

HERMIONE

> You gods, look down
> And from your sacred vials pour your graces
> Upon my daughter's head! Tell me, mine own.
150
> Where hast thou been preserved? where lived?
> how found
> Thy father's court? for thou shalt hear that I,
> Knowing by Paulina that the oracle
> Gave hope thou wast in being, have preserved
> Myself to see the issue.

PAULINA

155
> There's time enough for that;
> Lest they desire upon this push to trouble
> Your joys with like relation. Go together,
> You precious winners all; your exultation
> Partake to every one. I, an old turtle,
160
> Will wing me to some wither'd bough and there
> My mate, that's never to be found again,
> Lament till I am lost.

LEONTES

> O, peace, Paulina!
> Thou shouldst a husband take by my consent,

NO FEAR SHAKESPEARE

NO FEAR SHAKESPEARE

NO FEAR SHAKESPEARE

THE WINTER'S TALE

*sparknotes

Text © 2017 Sterling Publishing Co., Inc.
Cover © 2017 Sterling Publishing Co., Inc.

ISBN 978-1-4549-2806-5

Distributed in Canada by Sterling Publishing Co., Inc.
c/o Canadian Manda Group, 664 Annette Street
Toronto, Ontario M6S 2C8, Canada
Distributed in the United Kingdom by GMC Distribution Services
Castle Place, 166 High Street, Lewes, East Sussex BN7 1XU, England
Distributed in Australia by NewSouth Books
45 Beach Street, Coogee, NSW 2034, Australia

For information about custom editions, special sales, and premium
and corporate purchases, please contact Sterling Special Sales at
800-805-5489 or specialsales@sterlingpublishing.com.

Manufactured in the United States of America

Lot #:
2 4 6 8 10 9 7 5 3 1

10/17

sterlingpublishing.com
sparknotes.com

Cover and title page illustration by Richard Amari.

There's matter in these sighs, these profound heaves.
You must translate: 'tis fit we understand them.

(Hamlet, 4.1.1–2)

FEAR NOT.

Have you ever found yourself looking at a Shakespeare play, then down at the footnotes, then back up at the play, and still not understanding? You know what the individual words mean, but they don't add up. SparkNotes' *No Fear Shakespeare* will help you break through all that. Put the pieces together with our easy-to-read translations. Soon you'll be reading Shakespeare's own words fearlessly— and actually enjoying it.

No Fear Shakespeare puts Shakespeare's language side-by-side with a facing-page translation into modern English— the kind of English people actually speak today. When Shakespeare's words make your head spin, our translation will help you sort out what's happening, who's saying what, and why.

THE WINTER'S TALE

Characters ix

CHARACTERS

Leontes—The king of Sicilia and the childhood friend of
Polixenes. He is gripped by jealous fantasies that convince
him that Polixenes has been having an affair with his
wife, Hermione. His jealousy leads to the destruction of
his family.

Hermione—The virtuous and beautiful queen of Sicilia.
Falsely accused of infidelity by her husband, Leontes, she
apparently dies of grief just after being vindicated by the
oracle of Delphi. She is restored to life at the play's close.

Perdita—The daughter of Leontes and Hermione. Because
her father believes her to be illegitimate, she is abandoned
as a baby on the coast of Bohemia and brought up by a
shepherd. Unaware of her royal lineage, she falls in love
with the Bohemian prince, Florizel.

Polixenes—The king of Bohemia and Leontes's boyhood
friend. He is falsely accused of having an affair with
Leontes's wife and barely escapes Sicilia alive. Much later
in his life, he sees his only son fall in love with Perdita, who
has been living as a lowly shepherd's daughter.

Florizel—Polixenes's only son and heir. He falls in love with
Perdita, unaware of her royal ancestry, and defies his father
by eloping with her.

Camillo—An honest Sicilian nobleman. Camillo refuses to
follow Leontes's order to poison Polixenes, deciding
instead to flee Sicily and enter the Bohemian king's service.

Paulina—A noblewoman of Sicily. Paulina is fierce in her defense of Hermione's virtue and unrelenting in her condemnation of Leontes after Hermione's death. She is also the agent of the queen's resurrection.

Autolycus—A roguish peddler, vagabond, and pickpocket. He assists in Perdita and Florizel's escape.

The Shepherd—An old and honorable sheep tender. He finds Perdita as a baby and raises her as his own daughter.

Antigonus—Paulina's husband, and a loyal defender of Hermione. He is given the unfortunate task of abandoning the baby Perdita on the Bohemian coast.

The Clown—The shepherd's buffoonish son and Perdita's adopted brother.

Mamillius—Leontes and Hermione's son, the young prince of Sicilia. He dies, perhaps of grief, after his father wrongly imprisons his mother.

Cleomenes—A lord of Sicilia, sent to Delphi to ask the oracle about Hermione's guilt.

Dion—A Sicilian lord who accompanies Cleomenes to Delphi.

Emilia—One of Hermione's ladies-in-waiting.

Archidamus—A lord of Bohemia.

THE WINTER'S TALE

ACT ONE
SCENE 1

Antechamber in LEONTES' *palace.*
Enter CAMILLO *and* ARCHIDAMUS

ARCHIDAMUS

If you shall chance, Camillo, to visit Bohemia on the like
occasion whereon my services are now on foot, you shall
see, as I have said, great difference betwixt our Bohemia
and your Sicilia.

CAMILLO

5   I think, this coming summer, the King of Sicilia means to
pay Bohemia the visitation which he justly owes him.

ARCHIDAMUS

Wherein our entertainment shall shame us we will be
justified in our loves; for indeed—

CAMILLO

Beseech you,—

ARCHIDAMUS

10   Verily, I speak it in the freedom of my knowledge: we
cannot with such magnificence—in so rare—I know not
what to say. We will give you sleepy drinks, that your
senses, unintelligent of our insufficience, may, though
they cannot praise us, as little accuse us.

CAMILLO

15   You pay a great deal too dear for what's given freely.

ARCHIDAMUS

Believe me, I speak as my understanding instructs me
and as mine honesty puts it to utterance.

CAMILLO

Sicilia cannot show himself over-kind to Bohemia. They
were trained together in their childhoods; and there

ACT ONE
SCENE 1

A waiting room in LEONTES*'s palace.*
CAMILLO *and* ARCHIDAMUS *enter.*

ARCHIDAMUS
Camillo, if you ever happen to accompany your king to
Bohemia, as I am accompanying mine to Sicilia, you'll
see there's a great difference between our countries—and
our masters.

CAMILLO
I think the king of Sicilia plans to visit the king of
Bohemia this coming summer.

ARCHIDAMUS
If our hospitality is inadequate, we'll make up for it with
our love for you; in fact—

CAMILLO
Please—

ARCHIDAMUS
Truly, I say it from experience. We can't match the
magnificence, the excellence—I don't even know how to
describe it. We'll give you drinks to dull your senses, so
that you won't be aware of our inadequacies, and even if
you will be too sleepy to praise us, you won't be able to
accuse us of negligence either.

CAMILLO
You are putting too great a value on something that is
given for free.

ARCHIDAMUS
Believe me, I say what my knowledge tells me, and I say
it honestly.

CAMILLO
The king of Sicily could never be anything but kind to
the king of Bohemia. They were brought up together as

20 rooted betwixt them then such an affection, which cannot
choose but branch now. Since their more mature dignities
and royal necessities made separation of their society,
their encounters, though not personal, have been royally
attorneyed with interchange of gifts, letters, loving
25 embassies; that they have seemed to be together, though
absent, shook hands, as over a vast, and embraced, as
it were, from the ends of opposed winds. The heavens
continue their loves!

ARCHIDAMUS

I think there is not in the world either malice or matter
30 to alter it. You have an unspeakable comfort of your
young prince Mamillius: it is a gentleman of the greatest
promise that ever came into my note.

CAMILLO

I very well agree with you in the hopes of him: it is a
gallant child; one that indeed physics the subject, makes
35 old hearts fresh: they that went on crutches ere he was
born desire yet their life to see him a man.

ARCHIDAMUS

Would they else be content to die?

CAMILLO

Yes; if there were no other excuse why they should desire
to live.

ARCHIDAMUS

40 If the king had no son, they would desire to live on
crutches till he had one.

Exeunt

children, and so they have a deep-rooted affection for each other that can only grow. Because of their adult responsibilities and their duties as kings, they have not been able to meet personally. Instead, their meetings have taken place via royal deputies and through the exchange of presents, letters, and fond words. Through these means they've stayed in touch despite the great distance between them. May the heavens keep their friendship strong!

ARCHIDAMUS

I don't think there is anything in the world that can shake their friendship. And you have an indescribable comfort in the young Prince Mamillius. He has the greatest potential of any young gentleman I've ever seen.

CAMILLO

I agree with you regarding his potential. He is a noble child, and he is like a medicine for his subjects. The old feel young, and those who were crippled even before he was born now hope to live long enough to see him grow into a man.

ARCHIDAMUS

Would they otherwise want to die?

CAMILLO

Yes, if they didn't have any other reason to want to live.

ARCHIDAMUS

If the king didn't have a son, they would want to live as cripples until he had one.

They exit.

ACT 1, SCENE 2

A room of state in the same.
Enter LEONTES, HERMIONE, MAMILLIUS, POLIXENES,
CAMILLO, *and Attendants*

POLIXENES
    Nine changes of the watery star hath been
    The shepherd's note since we have left our throne
    Without a burthen: time as long again
    Would be filled up, my brother, with our thanks;
5   And yet we should, for perpetuity,
    Go hence in debt: and therefore, like a cipher,
    Yet standing in rich place, I multiply
    With one 'We thank you' many thousands more
    That go before it.

LEONTES
10   Stay your thanks a while;
    And pay them when you part.

POLIXENES
                   Sir, that's to-morrow.
    I am question'd by my fears, of what may chance
    Or breed upon our absence; that may blow
15   No sneaping winds at home, to make us say
    'This is put forth too truly:' besides, I have stay'd
    To tire your royalty.

LEONTES
              We are tougher, brother,
    Than you can put us to 't.

POLIXENES
20   No longer stay.

LEONTES
    One seven-night longer.

POLIXENES
              Very sooth, to-morrow.

ACT 1, SCENE 2

A formal receiving room in LEONTES's *palace.*
LEONTES, HERMIONE, MAMILLIUS, POLIXENES, CAMILLO,
and several Attendants enter.

POLIXENES

It has been nine months since I left my throne.
I could happily spend another nine months away, but
I must leave now, forever in your debt. So, like a zero,
which means "nothing" but adds value when
placed beside a number, my one "thank you" will
multiply the thousand more I've already said.

*For instance,
placing a
zero next to 1
makes it 10.*

LEONTES

Don't thank me yet. Wait until you leave.

POLIXENES

Sir, I leave tomorrow. I'm fearful of what might happen
by chance, or what plot may develop because of my
absence, and I worry that my fears will be confirmed.
Besides, I've worn you out with my company.

LEONTES

You couldn't wear me out if you tried.

POLIXENES

I can't stay any longer.

LEONTES

Just one more week.

POLIXENES

Really, tomorrow.

LEONTES

We'll part the time between 's then; and in that
I'll no gainsaying.

POLIXENES

25   Press me not, beseech you, so.
There is no tongue that moves, none, none i' the world,
So soon as yours could win me: so it should now,
Were there necessity in your request, although
'Twere needful I denied it. My affairs
30   Do even drag me homeward: which to hinder
Were in your love a whip to me; my stay
To you a charge and trouble: to save both,
Farewell, our brother.

LEONTES

Tongue-tied, our queen?
35   Speak you.

HERMIONE

I had thought, sir, to have held my peace until
You have drawn oaths from him not to stay. You, sir,
Charge him too coldly. Tell him, you are sure
All in Bohemia's well; this satisfaction
40   The by-gone day proclaim'd: say this to him,
He's beat from his best ward.

LEONTES

Well said, Hermione.

HERMIONE

To tell, he longs to see his son, were strong:
But let him say so then, and let him go;
45   But let him swear so, and he shall not stay,
We'll thwack him hence with distaffs.
Yet of your royal presence I'll adventure
The borrow of a week. When at Bohemia
You take my lord, I'll give him my commission
50   To let him there a month behind the gest
Prefix'd for 's parting: yet, good deed, Leontes,
I love thee not a jar o' the clock behind
What lady she her lord. You'll stay?

LEONTES

> We'll split the difference, and I won't hear
> any objections.

POLIXENES

> Please, don't plead with me. There is no one who can
> persuade me like you can, and you could persuade me
> to stay now if you really needed me to, even if it were
> necessary that I deny your request. My business does
> drag me home, so your attempts to keep me here, though
> done out of love, are painful to me. My staying only costs
> you and causes you trouble, so for both our sakes,
> I must go.

LEONTES

> My queen, are you mute? Speak.

HERMIONE

> I intended to keep quiet until you'd made him promise
> to stay. You argue too mildly. Tell him you are sure that
> things in Bohemia are fine—in fact, just the other day it
> was proclaimed so. Tell him this, and his best argument
> for leaving is gone.

LEONTES

> Well said, Hermione.

HERMIONE

> If he says that he wants to see his son, that's a strong
> argument. But let him say it first, then let him go. If
> he swears to that, he won't stay. We'll chase him off by
> whacking him with wooden staffs. But I'm guessing he
> will remain in your presence another week. (*to Polixenes*)
> When you receive my lord in Bohemia, I'll give him
> permission to stay a month past his fixed departure day.
> (*to Leontes*) Yet, Leontes, I don't love you a jot less than
> any other woman loves her lord. Polixenes, you'll stay?

POLIXENES

No, madam.

HERMIONE

55   Nay, but you will?

POLIXENES

I may not, verily.

HERMIONE

Verily!
You put me off with limber vows; but I,
Though you would seek to unsphere the stars with oaths,
60   Should yet say 'Sir, no going.' Verily,
You shall not go: a lady's 'Verily' 's
As potent as a lord's. Will you go yet?
Force me to keep you as a prisoner,
Not like a guest; so you shall pay your fees
65   When you depart, and save your thanks. How say you?
My prisoner? or my guest? by your dread 'Verily,'
One of them you shall be.

POLIXENES

Your guest, then, madam:
To be your prisoner should import offending;
70   Which is for me less easy to commit
Than you to punish.

HERMIONE

Not your gaoler, then,
But your kind hostess. Come, I'll question you
Of my lord's tricks and yours when you were boys:
75   You were pretty lordings then?

POLIXENES

We were, fair queen,
Two lads that thought there was no more behind
But such a day to-morrow as to-day,
And to be boy eternal.

HERMIONE

80   Was not my lord
The verier wag o' the two?

POLIXENES

No, madam.

HERMIONE

No, but you will?

POLIXENES

I can't, honestly.

HERMIONE

Honestly! You counter me with weak vows, but even if you would try to take the stars out of the sky with your oaths, I'll still say you are not going. Truly, you won't go—my "truly" is as powerful as yours. Will you still go? You'll force me to keep you like a prisoner, not like a guest, and you'll have to pay a fine at the end, rather than give us thanks. What do you think? My prisoner, or my guest? "Truly," as you say, you'll be one of the two.

POLIXENES

Your guest then, madam. Being your prisoner would suggest I've offended you, which would be more difficult and painful for me than your punishment.

HERMIONE

I won't be your jailer, then, but your kind hostess. Come, I'll ask you about the tricks you and my husband played when you were boys. You were handsome princes then?

POLIXENES

We were, fair queen, two young boys who thought that tomorrow would be just like today, and that we would be boys forever.

HERMIONE

Was my husband the bigger prankster of you two?

POLIXENES

We were as twinn'd lambs that did frisk i' the sun,
And bleat the one at the other: what we changed
Was innocence for innocence; we knew not
85 The doctrine of ill-doing, nor dream'd
That any did. Had we pursued that life,
And our weak spirits ne'er been higher rear'd
With stronger blood, we should have answer'd heaven
Boldly 'not guilty;' the imposition clear'd
90 Hereditary ours.

HERMIONE

By this we gather
You have tripp'd since.

POLIXENES

O my most sacred lady!
Temptations have since then been born to 's; for
95 In those unfledged days was my wife a girl;
Your precious self had then not cross'd the eyes
Of my young play-fellow.

HERMIONE

Grace to boot!
Of this make no conclusion, lest you say
100 Your queen and I are devils: yet go on;
The offences we have made you do we'll answer,
If you first sinn'd with us and that with us
You did continue fault and that you slipp'd not
With any but with us.

LEONTES

105 Is he won yet?

HERMIONE

He'll stay my lord.

LEONTES

At my request he would not.
Hermione, my dearest, thou never spokest
To better purpose.

POLIXENES

> We were like two lambs that played in the sun and
> bleated at one another. We were wholly innocent. We
> didn't know what it was to do harm, or even that anyone
> did. Had we continued this way, and had our weak spirits
> never given way to stronger passions, we could have said
> upon reaching Heaven that we were "not guilty," and we
> would have been cleared even of **original sin**.

The doctrine that all people are born tainted by sin because the first humans, Adam and Eve, disobeyed God.

HERMIONE

> I take it that you have not been so innocent since?

POLIXENES

> Most sacred lady! We've had our temptations since then.
> In those youthful days my wife was just a girl, and my
> playfellow had not yet seen you.

HERMIONE

> Heaven help me! Don't pursue that train of thought,
> or you'll go on to say that your wife and I are devils.
> Still, keep going. We'll take responsibility for whatever
> sins we've made you commit, as long as those sins were
> committed first with us, only with us, and you've never
> sinned with any other.

LEONTES

> Is he won over yet?

HERMIONE

> He'll stay, my lord.

LEONTES

> When I requested it he would not. Hermione, my
> dearest, you've never spoken so well.

HERMIONE

110   Never?

LEONTES

                                    Never, but once.

HERMIONE

What! have I twice said well? when was 't before?
I prithee tell me; cram 's with praise, and make 's
As fat as tame things: one good deed dying tongueless
115   Slaughters a thousand waiting upon that.
Our praises are our wages: you may ride 's
With one soft kiss a thousand furlongs ere
With spur we beat an acre. But to the goal:
My last good deed was to entreat his stay:
120   What was my first? it has an elder sister,
Or I mistake you: O, would her name were Grace!
But once before I spoke to the purpose: when?
Nay, let me have 't; I long.

LEONTES

                                    Why, that was when
125   Three crabbed months had sour'd themselves to death,
Ere I could make thee open thy white hand
And clap thyself my love: then didst thou utter
'I am yours for ever.'

HERMIONE

                          'Tis grace indeed.
130   Why, lo you now, I have spoke to the purpose twice:
The one for ever earn'd a royal husband;
The other for some while a friend.

LEONTES

                          (*aside*) Too hot, too hot!
To mingle friendship far is mingling bloods.
135   I have tremor cordis on me: my heart dances;
But not for joy; not joy. This entertainment
May a free face put on, derive a liberty
From heartiness, from bounty, fertile bosom,
And well become the agent; 't may, I grant;

HERMIONE

Never?

LEONTES

Only once before.

HERMIONE

What! I've only spoken well twice? When was the last time? Please, tell me. Fill me up with praise and make me as fat as a pet. If one good deed goes unrecognized, the thousand more that might have been inspired by it will never occur. Praise is our motivation and reward. One soft kiss will take you two hundred yards; a sharp kick only gets you an acre. But back to the point: my last good deed was to plead for Polixenes to stay. What was my first good deed? Unless I'm misunderstanding what you said, there was an earlier one. Oh, if only my name were Grace! So once before I've spoken well. When? Tell me, please, I long to know.

LEONTES

Why, it was when three bitter months had passed before I could get you to pledge your love to me with your white hands. And then you said, "I am yours forever."

HERMIONE

It is grace, indeed. According to you, I have spoken well twice: once to earn a royal husband and again to keep a **friend** a while longer.

LEONTES

(*aside*) That is too much! To take friendship too far is to make it a love affair. My heart is trembling and dancing, but not for joy. This hospitality may have an innocent face, and my wife's generosity may in fact come from warmth, affection, and the fact that it makes her more attractive. Maybe. But to hold hands, as they are doing right now, and flirtatiously

The word "friend" could also mean lover, a meaning Leontes refers to in the speech that follows.

140 But to be paddling palms and pinching fingers,
As now they are, and making practised smiles,
As in a looking-glass, and then to sigh, as 'twere
The mort o' the deer; O, that is entertainment
My bosom likes not, nor my brows! Mamillius,
145 Art thou my boy?

MAMILLIUS

Ay, my good lord.

LEONTES

I' fecks!
Why, that's my bawcock. What, hast smutch'd thy nose?
They say it is a copy out of mine. Come, captain,
150 We must be neat; not neat, but cleanly, captain:
And yet the steer, the heifer and the calf
Are all call'd neat.—Still virginalling
Upon his palm!—How now, you wanton calf!
Art thou my calf?

MAMILLIUS

155 Yes, if you will, my lord.

LEONTES

Thou want'st a rough pash and the shoots that I have,
To be full like me: yet they say we are
Almost as like as eggs; women say so,
That will say anything but were they false
160 As o'er-dyed blacks, as wind, as waters, false
As dice are to be wish'd by one that fixes
No bourn 'twixt his and mine, yet were it true
To say this boy were like me. Come, sir page,
Look on me with your welkin eye: sweet villain!
165 Most dear'st! my collop! Can thy dam?—may 't be?—
Affection! thy intention stabs the centre:
Thou dost make possible things not so held,
Communicatest with dreams;—how can this be?—
With what's unreal thou coactive art,
170 And fellow'st nothing: then 'tis very credent
Thou mayst co-join with something; and thou dost,

smile at each other as though into a mirror, a
while sighing as loud as a **horn blast**, that is
entertainment that pleases my heart, or my hea
Mamillius, are you my son?

...of a
...nted deer.

MAMILLIUS

Yes, my good lord.

LEONTES

In faith! That's my fine fellow. What, have you
smudged your nose? They say it looks just like mine.
Come on, captain, you must be **neat**, that is, clean.
Yet the steer, the heifer, and the calf are all called
neat. Still playing her fingers up and down his palm!
What are you up to, you silly calf? Are you my calf?

The term refers
to cattle with
horns, leading
to Leontes's
comment in the
next sentence.

MAMILLIUS

Yes, if you'd like me to be, my lord.

LEONTES

You need a shaggy head and **horns** to be just like
me. Still, they say we are as alike as a pair of eggs.
Women say that, and they will say anything. But
even if they were **as false as Africans or black
fabric**, or as fickle as the wind and the water, or
fixed as a cheating gambler wants the dice to be,
it would still be true that this boy looks like me.
Come, sir page, look at me with your sky-blue eye.
Sweet villain! Dearest! My flesh! Can your mother
have? Could it be? Jealousy's intensity strikes me
through to my heart and makes things that are
impossible seem possible. That jealousy speaks
in dreams. How can this be? It collaborates with
what's unreal and corresponds to nothing in real
life. Then it's very believable that my jealousy may
be real, and she's gone beyond what's permitted,

Men whose
wives have been
unfaithful, or
cuckolds, were
often depicted
with horns.

A common belief
at the time was
that Africans
were sexually
promiscuous
and thus "false"
in that they
weren't faithful.
Black fabric,
meanwhile,
became weak, or
"false," as a result
of the chemicals
used to make
the black dye.

POLIXENES

175   What means Sicilia?

HERMIONE

He something seems unsettled.

POLIXENES

How, my lord?

LEONTES

What cheer? how is 't with you, best brother?

HERMIONE

You look as if you held a brow of much distraction
180   Are you moved, my lord?

LEONTES

No, in good earnest.
How sometimes nature will betray its folly,
Its tenderness, and make itself a pastime
To harder bosoms! Looking on the lines
185   Of my boy's face, methoughts I did recoil
Twenty-three years, and saw myself unbreech'd,
In my green velvet coat, my dagger muzzled,
Lest it should bite its master, and so prove,
As ornaments oft do, too dangerous:
190   How like, methought, I then was to this kernel,
This squash, this gentleman. Mine honest friend,
Will you take eggs for money?

MAMILLIUS

No, my lord, I'll fight.

LEONTES

You will! why, happy man be 's dole! My brother,
195   Are you so fond of your young prince as we
Do seem to be of ours?

POLIXENES

If at home, sir,
He's all my exercise, my mirth, my matter,

and I would find out and grow insane, and my brow would harden into horns.

POLIXENES

What is Leontes saying?

HERMIONE

He seems upset.

POLIXENES

How are you, my lord?

LEONTES

What news? How are you, my best brother?

HERMIONE

You look distracted. Are you upset, my lord?

LEONTES

No, truly. Sometimes nature shows its weakness, its tenderness, and makes itself a source of amusement for harder hearts. Looking at my boy's face, I thought I had gone back twenty-three years and saw myself **without trousers**, in my green velvet coat, with my dagger carefully sheathed so I would not hurt myself on it and so it wouldn't prove too dangerous, as toys often do. I thought how alike I was at that age to this child, this young boy, this gentleman. My honest friend, will you accept something relatively worthless in exchange for something valuable?

> Leontes means he saw himself as a young boy who was not yet wearing men's clothing. In England at the time, boys younger than six were dressed in gowns. Putting a boy in trousers, or breeches, signified the boy's transition out of childhood.

MAMILLIUS

No, my lord, I'll fight.

LEONTES

You will! May happiness be his fortune! My brother, are you as fond of your young prince as I seem to be of mine?

POLIXENES

When I'm home, sir, he's my occupation, my laughter, all I worry about. First he's my sworn friend, then he's

Now my sworn friend and then mine enemy,
200   My parasite, my soldier, statesman, all:
He makes a July's day short as December,
And with his varying childness cures in me
Thoughts that would thick my blood.

LEONTES

So stands this squire
205   Officed with me: we two will walk, my lord,
And leave you to your graver steps. Hermione,
How thou lovest us, show in our brother's welcome;
Let what is dear in Sicily be cheap:
Next to thyself and my young rover, he's
210   Apparent to my heart.

HERMIONE

If you would seek us,
We are yours i' the garden: shall 's attend you there?

LEONTES

To your own bents dispose you: you'll be found,
Be you beneath the sky.
215   (*aside*) I am angling now,
Though you perceive me not how I give line.
Go to, go to!
How she holds up the neb, the bill to him!
And arms her with the boldness of a wife
220   To her allowing husband!

Exeunt POLIXENES, HERMIONE, *and Attendants*

Gone already!
Inch-thick, knee-deep, o'er head and ears a fork'd one!
Go, play, boy, play: thy mother plays, and I
Play too, but so disgraced a part, whose issue
225   Will hiss me to my grave: contempt and clamour
Will be my knell. Go, play, boy, play. There have been,
Or I am much deceived, cuckolds ere now;
And many a man there is, even at this present,
Now while I speak this, holds his wife by the arm,

an enemy, a freeloader, a soldier, and a states
together. He makes a long summer's day feel a
day in the middle of winter. And his childish w
me from gloomy thoughts.

LEONTES

This young squire here does the same for me. He and ı
will walk along, my lord, and leave you to your slower
steps. Hermione, show how much you love us in how you
entertain our brother. Give him whatever he wants, no
matter how expensive. After you and my young son, he's
dearest to me.

HERMIONE

If you are looking for us, we'll be in the garden. Should
we wait for you there?

LEONTES

Do whatever pleases you. I'll find you, if you are
anywhere under the sky. (*aside*) I'm fishing now, though
no one sees how I set the line. Go on! Look how she holds
up her nose and mouth to him, as if to be kissed. She acts
with the boldness of a wife toward her husband!

> **POLIXENES, HERMIONE,** *and Attendants exit.*

Gone already! A little here, knee-deep there, then grow
horns over my head and behind my ears! Go, boy, play.
Your mother plays around, and I play a role, though my
part is one of a disgrace, with the result that I'll be hissed
on my way to the grave, with contempt as my funeral
bells. Go play, boy, play. Unless I'm mistaken, there
have been cuckolds before. Even now, as I speak, there is
many a man who may hold his wife by the arm without
suspecting that she has been unfaithful in his absence,

230 That little thinks she has been sluiced in 's absence
And his pond fish'd by his next neighbour, by
Sir Smile, his neighbour: nay, there's comfort in 't
Whiles other men have gates and those gates open'd,
As mine, against their will. Should all despair
235 That have revolted wives, the tenth of mankind
Would hang themselves. Physic for 't there is none;
It is a bawdy planet, that will strike
Where 'tis predominant; and 'tis powerful, think it,
From east, west, north and south: be it concluded,
240 No barricado for a belly; know 't;
It will let in and out the enemy
With bag and baggage: many thousand on 's
Have the disease, and feel 't not. How now, boy!

MAMILLIUS
I am like you, they say.

LEONTES
245   Why that's some comfort.
What, Camillo there?

CAMILLO
Ay, my good lord.

LEONTES
Go play, Mamillius; thou 'rt an honest man.

                                        Exit MAMILLIUS

Camillo, this great sir will yet stay longer.

CAMILLO
250 You had much ado to make his anchor hold:
When you cast out, it still came home.

LEONTES
                                        Didst note it?

CAMILLO
He would not stay at your petitions: made
His business more material.

and his neighbor, call him Sir Smile, has been with t
woman that belongs to him. There's comfort in the f
that other men have had wives and those wives have l
unfaithful, as mine has, against their will. If everyone
whose wife strayed were to despair, a tenth of mankind
would hang themselves. There's no remedy for it, since
it is a world full of lust, from east to west and north and
south. There's no barricade you can build around the
womb, and one's enemy will go in and out as he pleases.
Thousands of us have the disease and don't know it.
What now, boy?

MAMILLIUS

I look like you, they say.

LEONTES

That's some comfort. Camillo, are you there?

CAMILLO

Yes, my good lord.

LEONTES

Go play, Mamillius, that's a good boy.

MAMILLIUS *exits.*

Camillo, my friend Polixenes will stay longer.

CAMILLO

You had to go to great lengths to make him stay.
No matter what you said, he insisted he would leave.

LEONTES

Did you see it?

CAMILLO

He wouldn't heed your pleas, but said his business was
too important.

LEONTES

255   Didst perceive it?
        (*aside*) They're here with me already,
                whispering, rounding
        'Sicilia is a so-forth:' 'tis far gone,
        When I shall gust it last. How came 't, Camillo,
260   That he did stay?

CAMILLO

                        At the good queen's entreaty.

LEONTES

        At the queen's be 't: 'good' should be pertinent
        But, so it is, it is not. Was this taken
        By any understanding pate but thine?
265   For thy conceit is soaking, will draw in
        More than the common blocks: not noted, is 't,
        But of the finer natures? by some severals
        Of head-piece extraordinary? lower messes
        Perchance are to this business purblind? say.

CAMILLO

270   Business, my lord? I think most understand
        Bohemia stays here longer.

LEONTES
        Ha?

CAMILLO

        Stays here longer.

LEONTES

                                Ay, but why?

CAMILLO

275   To satisfy your highness and the entreaties
        Of our most gracious mistress.

LEONTES

                                Satisfy!
        The entreaties of your mistress! satisfy!
        Let that suffice. I have trusted thee, Camillo,
280   With all the nearest things to my heart, as well
        My chamber-councils, wherein, priest-like, thou

LEONTES

You saw it? (*aside*) People know my secret already, and they are whispering and murmuring, "Sicilia is a such-and-such." It is already so well-known while I am just figuring it out. Camillo, how did it happen that he stayed?

CAMILLO

Because the good queen asked him.

LEONTES

True, because of the queen. "Good" should be an appropriate description, but under the circumstances it isn't. Did anyone else see that it happened this way? Since you notice more than the common idiots, perhaps it is only seen by those intelligent enough, the ones with extraordinary intellects? Perhaps the commoners are blind to what just happened? Tell me.

CAMILLO

What happened, my lord? I think almost everyone understands that Polixenes will stay here longer.

LEONTES

What?

CAMILLO

He will stay here longer.

LEONTES

But why?

CAMILLO

To satisfy your highness and the request of our most gracious mistress.

LEONTES

Satisfy! The request of your mistress! Satisfy her! That's enough. I have trusted you, Camillo, with everything dearest to my heart, as well as confessed to you in my chamber. I parted from you there feeling repentant and reformed, as though departing from a visit to a priest.

Hast cleansed my bosom, I from thee departed
Thy penitent reform'd: but we have been
Deceived in thy integrity, deceived
285   In that which seems so.

CAMILLO

                                 Be it forbid, my lord!

LEONTES

To bide upon 't, thou art not honest, or,
If thou inclinest that way, thou art a coward,
Which hoxes honesty behind, restraining
290   From course required; or else thou must be counted
A servant grafted in my serious trust
And therein negligent; or else a fool
That seest a game play'd home, the rich stake drawn,
And takest it all for jest.

CAMILLO

295   My gracious lord,
I may be negligent, foolish and fearful;
In every one of these no man is free,
But that his negligence, his folly, fear,
Among the infinite doings of the world,
300   Sometime puts forth. In your affairs, my lord,
If ever I were wilful-negligent,
It was my folly; if industriously
I play'd the fool, it was my negligence,
Not weighing well the end; if ever fearful
305   To do a thing, where I the issue doubted,
Where of the execution did cry out
Against the non-performance, 'twas a fear
Which oft infects the wisest: these, my lord,
Are such allow'd infirmities that honesty
310   Is never free of. But, beseech your grace,
Be plainer with me; let me know my trespass
By its own visage: if I then deny it,
'Tis none of mine.

But now I feel that I have been deceived by what appears to be your integrity.

CAMILLO

Forbid the thought, my lord!

LEONTES

Now that I think of it, you are either dishonest or, if you are honest, you are a coward, hiding your honesty for fear of having to follow the correct course of action. Perhaps you neglect your duties as a most trusted servant, or perhaps you are a fool who sees the high stakes of a game but thinks it's all a joke.

CAMILLO

My gracious lord, I may be negligent, foolish, and cowardly. No man is free from all those vices, and they will occasionally turn up. In your affairs, my lord, if I was ever deliberately negligent, it was because of my foolishness. If I ever pretended to be a fool, it was because of my neglectfulness and my inability to judge the consequences. If ever I was afraid to do something when I was uncertain of the outcome—and the deed was so necessary it had to be done—it was a fear that even wise men feel. My lord, these are acceptable weaknesses that honesty is always plagued by. But I beg your grace to be blunt: tell me exactly what I did wrong. Then if I deny that I did it, it truly is not my fault.

LEONTES

315   Ha' not you seen, Camillo,—
But that's past doubt, you have, or your eye-glass
Is thicker than a cuckold's horn,—or heard,—
For to a vision so apparent rumour
Cannot be mute,—or thought,—for cogitation
Resides not in that man that does not think,—
320 My wife is slippery? If thou wilt confess,
Or else be impudently negative,
To have nor eyes nor ears nor thought, then say
My wife's a hobby-horse, deserves a name
As rank as any flax-wench that puts to
325 Before her troth-plight: say 't and justify 't.

CAMILLO

I would not be a stander-by to hear
My sovereign mistress clouded so, without
My present vengeance taken: 'shrew my heart,
You never spoke what did become you less
330 Than this; which to reiterate were sin
As deep as that, though true.

LEONTES

                         Is whispering nothing?
Is leaning cheek to cheek? is meeting noses?
Kissing with inside lip? stopping the career
335 Of laughing with a sigh?—a note infallible
Of breaking honesty—horsing foot on foot?
Skulking in corners? wishing clocks more swift?
Hours, minutes? noon, midnight? and all eyes
Blind with the pin and web but theirs, theirs only,
340 That would unseen be wicked? is this nothing?
Why, then the world and all that's in 't is nothing;
The covering sky is nothing; Bohemia nothing;
My wife is nothing; nor nothing have these nothings,
If this be nothing.

The Winter's T

LEONTES

Haven't you seen? You have, that's not in
you are willfully blind. Or perhaps you h
rumors can't be mute in the face of someth.
Or maybe you have thought, since every man
must have thought it. Isn't my wife deceiving me: ૫૦.
must confess, unless you want to shamelessly deny that
you have either eyes or ears or thought, that my wife is a
whore, and deserves a name as awful as any base woman
deserves who sleeps with a man before she is married. Say
it and affirm it.

CAMILLO

I wouldn't stand by and listen to my mistress be
slandered like that without taking revenge immediately.
Curse my heart, I've never heard you speak in a way that
suited you less. To say it again would be as sinful as the
crime you are describing, even if it was true.

LEONTES

Is it nothing that they whisper together? Lean their
cheeks together? Or touch noses? Or kisses? Or interrupt
their laughter with sighs, a certain sign that they're in
love? Or playing footsie? Or lurking in corners? Or
wishing that time would run faster, that hours were
minutes and noon midnight, and that all eyes were blind
with cataracts but theirs, so that they can be wicked
without being seen? Is this nothing? Why, then the
world and everything in it is nothing. The sky is nothing,
Polixenes is nothing, my wife is nothing, and they have
nothing, if this is nothing.

CAMILLO

45   Good my lord, be cured
Of this diseased opinion, and betimes;
For 'tis most dangerous.

LEONTES
                                        Say it be, 'tis true.

CAMILLO
No, no, my lord.

LEONTES
350   It is; you lie, you lie:
I say thou liest, Camillo, and I hate thee,
Pronounce thee a gross lout, a mindless slave,
Or else a hovering temporizer, that
Canst with thine eyes at once see good and evil,
355   Inclining to them both: were my wife's liver
Infected as her life, she would not live
The running of one glass.

CAMILLO
                                        Who does infect her?

LEONTES
Why, he that wears her like a medal, hanging
360   About his neck, Bohemia: who, if I
Had servants true about me, that bare eyes
To see alike mine honour as their profits,
Their own particular thrifts, they would do that
Which should undo more doing: ay, and thou,
365   His cupbearer,—whom I from meaner form
Have benched and reared to worship, who mayst see
Plainly as heaven sees earth and earth sees heaven,
How I am galled,—mightst bespice a cup,
To give mine enemy a lasting wink;
370   Which draught to me were cordial.

CAMILLO
                                        Sir, my lord,
I could do this, and that with no rash potion,
But with a lingering dram that should not work

CAMILLO

> My lord, let go of this terrible opinion, and quickly, because it is dangerous.

LEONTES

> Say it is, for it is true.

CAMILLO

> No, no, my lord.

LEONTES

> It is true, and you lie. I say you lie, Camillo, and I hate you. I call you a horrible oaf, a mindless slave, or else nervous and wishy-washy, who's able to see good and evil in the same thing and is inclined to both. If my wife were as diseased physically as she is morally, she wouldn't survive an hour.

CAMILLO

> Who corrupts her?

LEONTES

> The one who wears her like a medal around his neck: Polixenes. If I had loyal servants who saw my honor as their business and personal gain, they would act to prevent any more of this affair. And you, his **cupbearer**—I brought you up from a low rank, have given you some authority, and brought you up to respectability. You should be able to see plainly how upset I am. You could poison his drink to kill him, which would make me feel better.

The man who served wine to the master in a noble household.

CAMILLO

> My lord, I could do it with a tiny amount of a slow-working potion that isn't as violent as poison. But I can't believe that my noble mistress would be so flawed,

Maliciously like poison: but I cannot
375   Believe this crack to be in my dread mistress,
So sovereignly being honourable.
I have loved thee,—

LEONTES

Make that thy question, and go rot!
Dost think I am so muddy, so unsettled,
380   To appoint myself in this vexation, sully
The purity and whiteness of my sheets,
Which to preserve is sleep, which being spotted
Is goads, thorns, nettles, tails of wasps,
Give scandal to the blood o' the prince my son,
385   Who I do think is mine and love as mine,
Without ripe moving to 't? Would I do this?
Could man so blench?

CAMILLO

                  I must believe you, sir:
I do; and will fetch off Bohemia for 't;
390   Provided that, when he's removed, your highness
Will take again your queen as yours at first,
Even for your son's sake; and thereby for sealing
The injury of tongues in courts and kingdoms
Known and allied to yours.

LEONTES

395   Thou dost advise me
Even so as I mine own course have set down:
I'll give no blemish to her honour, none.

CAMILLO

                        My lord,
Go then; and with a countenance as clear
400   As friendship wears at feasts, keep with Bohemia
And with your queen. I am his cupbearer:
If from me he have wholesome beverage,
Account me not your servant.

having shown herself always so honorable. I have loved you—

LEONTES

Make that your problem, and go to hell! Do you think I am so dull-witted, so unsettled, that I would give myself all this trouble and dirty up the pure, clean whiteness of my bed? To preserve that purity gives one peace of mind, but if it's tainted it hurts like thorns, nettles, and wasp stings. Do you think I would raise doubt about the legitimacy of my son, who I believe is mine and who I love, without compelling reasons? Would I do this? Could I turn aside from this?

CAMILLO

I must believe you, sir, and I do. I'll take care of Polixenes for you, as long as once he's gone you will again treat your wife as your own, at least for your son's sake. That way you will silence all the harmful rumors that might spread to other kingdoms and courts that are allied with you.

LEONTES

You advise me to do what I already determined I would do. I won't tarnish her reputation in any way.

CAMILLO

My lord, then go, and with a face as open and friendly as if you were at a party, keep company with Polixenes and your queen. I am his cupbearer, and I will give him the potion, or no longer think of me as your servant.

LEONTES

                    This is all:
405   Do 't and thou hast the one half of my heart;
       Do 't not, thou split'st thine own.

CAMILLO

                                    I'll do 't, my lord.

LEONTES

       I will seem friendly, as thou hast advised me.

                                                Exeunt

CAMILLO

       O miserable lady! But, for me,
410   What case stand I in? I must be the poisoner
       Of good Polixenes; and my ground to do 't
       Is the obedience to a master, one
       Who in rebellion with himself will have
       All that are his so too. To do this deed,
415   Promotion follows. If I could find example
       Of thousands that had struck anointed kings
       And flourish'd after, I'd not do 't; but since
       Nor brass nor stone nor parchment bears not one,
       Let villany itself forswear 't. I must
420   Forsake the court: to do 't, or no, is certain
       To me a break-neck. Happy star, reign now!
       Here comes Bohemia.

       Re-enter POLIXENES

POLIXENES

                        This is strange: methinks
       My favour here begins to warp. Not speak?
425   Good day, Camillo.

CAMILLO

                        Hail, most royal sir!

POLIXENES

       What is the news i' the court?

LEONTES

> Do this and you will have one half of my heart. Don't do it, and your own will be split.

CAMILLO

> I'll do it, my lord.

LEONTES

> I'll act friendly, as you've advised me.

> > *LEONTES exits.*

CAMILLO

> Oh, unfortunate lady! What have I gotten into? I have to poison good Polixenes, only because I would obey a master who is mad and wants all his servants to be mad, too. If I do this, I'll be promoted. But even if I could find one example of someone who had struck down a chosen king and prospered, I wouldn't do it. Since there isn't such an example recorded anywhere in history, even a villain wouldn't do it. I have to leave the court, since whether I do it or not I'm certain to be hanged. Oh, good! Here comes Polixenes.

> *POLIXENES reenters.*

POLIXENES

> This is odd. I think I'm losing favor here. He wouldn't speak? Good day, Camillo.

CAMILLO

> Hello, most royal sir!

POLIXENES

> What is the news of the court?

CAMILLO

               None rare, my lord.

POLIXENES

    The king hath on him such a countenance

430   As he had lost some province and a region

    Loved as he loves himself: even now I met him

    With customary compliment; when he,

    Wafting his eyes to the contrary and falling

    A lip of much contempt, speeds from me and

435   So leaves me to consider what is breeding

    That changeth thus his manners.

CAMILLO

             I dare not know, my lord.

POLIXENES

    How! dare not! do not. Do you know, and dare not?

    Be intelligent to me: 'tis thereabouts;

440   For, to yourself, what you do know, you must.

    And cannot say, you dare not. Good Camillo,

    Your changed complexions are to me a mirror

    Which shows me mine changed too; for I must be

    A party in this alteration, finding

445   Myself thus alter'd with 't.

CAMILLO

           There is a sickness

    Which puts some of us in distemper, but

    I cannot name the disease; and it is caught

    Of you that yet are well.

POLIXENES

450   How! caught of me!

    Make me not sighted like the basilisk:

    I have look'd on thousands, who have sped the better

    By my regard, but kill'd none so. Camillo,—

    As you are certainly a gentleman, thereto

455   Clerk-like experienced, which no less adorns

    Our gentry than our parents' noble names,

    In whose success we are gentle,—I beseech you,

CAMILLO

Nothing unusual, my lord.

POLIXENES

The king looked as though he had lost a part of his kingdom as dear to him as himself. Just now I met him with the usual cordial greetings, but, turning his eyes away and sneering in contempt, he walked away from me, leaving me to wonder what happened to make him act this way.

CAMILLO

I don't dare know, my lord.

POLIXENES

What? You don't dare, or you don't know? Do you know, but don't dare? It must be something of the sort, because if you know something for certain, you can't deny it. Good Camillo, your face is like a mirror to me, in which your changed expression shows my own. I must be responsible in some way for Leontes's altered behavior, since I'm changed, too.

CAMILLO

There is an illness that makes some of us mad, but I can't say exactly what it is. But even though you are still well, you have caught it, too.

POLIXENES

What do you mean, I've caught it, too? Don't tell me I have the deadly stare of the **basilisk**. I've looked at thousands of people who have been better off by having been seen by me, but I've never killed anyone that way. Camillo, I know you are a gentleman because you are educated, and that makes one a gentleman as much as having parents who are nobles. I beg you, if you know something I should

A mythical reptile that was able to kill with its stare.

If you know aught which does behove my knowledge
Thereof to be inform'd, imprison 't not
460   In ignorant concealment.

CAMILLO
                                   I may not answer.

POLIXENES
A sickness caught of me, and yet I well!
I must be answer'd. Dost thou hear, Camillo,
I conjure thee, by all the parts of man
465   Which honour does acknowledge, whereof the least
Is not this suit of mine, that thou declare
What incidency thou dost guess of harm
Is creeping toward me; how far off, how near;
Which way to be prevented, if to be;
470   If not, how best to bear it.

CAMILLO
                                   Sir, I will tell you;
Since I am charged in honour and by him
That I think honourable: therefore mark my counsel,
Which must be even as swiftly follow'd as
475   I mean to utter it, or both yourself and me
Cry lost, and so good night!

POLIXENES
                                   On, good Camillo.

CAMILLO
I am appointed him to murder you.

POLIXENES
By whom, Camillo?

CAMILLO
480   By the king.

POLIXENES
                                   For what?

CAMILLO
He thinks, nay, with all confidence he swears,
As he had seen 't or been an instrument
To vice you to 't, that you have touch'd his queen
485   Forbiddenly.

know, please don't pretend not to know and keep it
from me.

CAMILLO

I can't tell you.

POLIXENES

I've caught an illness, even though I am well! You have to
tell me. Do you hear me, Camillo? I appeal to you by all
the traits in a man that respond to honor, including this
request itself. Tell me why you think I'm in danger, how
close the danger is, and how I might prevent it. Or if I
can't, how I might best endure it.

CAMILLO

Sir, I will tell you, since I am obligated by my honor and
since you're an honorable man. Therefore listen to my
advice, which must be followed immediately, or both you
and I will be doomed and will meet a bad end.

POLIXENES

Go ahead, good Camillo.

CAMILLO

I have been appointed by him to murder you.

POLIXENES

By whom, Camillo?

CAMILLO

By the king.

POLIXENES

Why?

CAMILLO

He thinks, no, he swears with as much confidence as if
he had seen it or even helped you do it, that you have
touched his queen in a forbidden way.

POLIXENES
> O, then my best blood turn
> To an infected jelly and my name
> Be yoked with his that did betray the Best!
> Turn then my freshest reputation to
490 A savour that may strike the dullest nostril
> Where I arrive, and my approach be shunn'd,
> Nay, hated too, worse than the great'st infection
> That e'er was heard or read!

CAMILLO
>   Swear his thought over
495 By each particular star in heaven and
> By all their influences, you may as well
> Forbid the sea for to obey the moon
> As or by oath remove or counsel shake
> The fabric of his folly, whose foundation
500 Is piled upon his faith and will continue
> The standing of his body.

POLIXENES
>   How should this grow?

CAMILLO
> I know not: but I am sure 'tis safer to
> Avoid what's grown than question how 'tis born.
505 If therefore you dare trust my honesty,
> That lies enclosed in this trunk which you
> Shall bear along impawn'd, away to-night!
> Your followers I will whisper to the business,
> And will by twos and threes at several posterns
510 Clear them o' the city. For myself, I'll put
> My fortunes to your service, which are here
> By this discovery lost. Be not uncertain;
> For, by the honour of my parents, I
> Have utter'd truth: which if you seek to prove,
515 I dare not stand by; nor shall you be safer
> Than one condemn'd by the king's own mouth, thereon
> His execution sworn.

POLIXENES

If I did, may my blood turn to poison and my name
be as despised as Judas's! Let my reputation rot and
stink so badly that even the least sensitive nose will be
overwhelmed, and when I approach they'll turn their
backs! Let me be hated more than the worst disease that
has ever been heard of!

CAMILLO

No matter how vehemently you swear his suspicions
aren't true, you are as likely to keep the sea from obeying
the moon as you are to change his mind. Neither will
oaths or wise words disturb the foundation of his foolish
notion, which is built on his faith and will last for the rest
of his life.

POLIXENES

How did this come about?

CAMILLO

I don't know, but I'm sure it's safer to avoid his jealousy
than to wonder why he feels that way. So if you trust my
honesty, which you shall take as my pledge, then leave
tonight! I'll quietly let your followers know and get them
out of the back gates of the city two or three at a time.
As for me, I've lost everything I have by revealing this
to you, but I'll put what I have to your service. Don't be
uncertain. By the honor of my parents, I'm telling the
truth. If you try to prove it, I'll deny I ever said it. You
won't be any safer than a man whom the king himself has
condemned to be executed.

POLIXENES

                     I do believe thee:
I saw his heart in 's face. Give me thy hand:
520   Be pilot to me and thy places shall
Still neighbour mine. My ships are ready and
My people did expect my hence departure
Two days ago. This jealousy
Is for a precious creature: as she's rare,
525   Must it be great, and as his person's mighty,
Must it be violent, and as he does conceive
He is dishonour'd by a man which ever
Profess'd to him, why, his revenges must
In that be made more bitter. Fear o'ershades me:
530   Good expedition be my friend, and comfort
The gracious queen, part of his theme, but nothing
Of his ill-ta'en suspicion! Come, Camillo;
I will respect thee as a father if
Thou bear'st my life off hence: let us avoid.

CAMILLO

535   It is in mine authority to command
To take the urgent hour. Come, sir, away.

Exeunt

POLIXENES

> I do believe you. I saw what he felt in his face. Give
> me your hand. Guide me and our fortunes will remain
> together. My ships are ready, and my people expected me
> to depart two days ago. He's jealous over a very precious
> woman, and so his jealousy will be as great as she is rare,
> and as violent as he is powerful. And since he thinks that
> a man who always professed friendship has deceived him,
> his revenge will be even more bitter. I'm overwhelmed
> with fear. May my swift exit help me, and may it comfort
> the good queen, who has no responsibility for his
> unjustified suspicions. Come, Camillo. I will respect you
> like a father if you take me away safely. Let us leave.

CAMILLO

> I have the authority to pass through all the back gates of
> the city. Let's go soon. Come, sir, let's leave.
>
> *They exit.*

ACT TWO
SCENE 1

A room in LEONTES' *palace.*
Enter HERMIONE, MAMILLIUS, *and Ladies*

HERMIONE
>Take the boy to you: he so troubles me,
>'Tis past enduring.

FIRST LADY
>   Come, my gracious lord,
>Shall I be your playfellow?

MAMILLIUS
5   No, I'll none of you.

FIRST LADY
>   Why, my sweet lord?

MAMILLIUS
>You'll kiss me hard and speak to me as if
>I were a baby still. I love you better.

SECOND LADY
>And why so, my lord?

MAMILLIUS
10   Not for because
>Your brows are blacker; yet black brows, they say,
>Become some women best, so that there be not
>Too much hair there, but in a semicircle
>Or a half-moon made with a pen.

SECOND LADY
15   Who taught you this?

MAMILLIUS
>I learnt it out of women's faces. Pray now
>What colour are your eyebrows?

FIRST LADY
>   Blue, my lord.

ACT TWO
SCENE 1

A room in LEONTES'*s palace.*
HERMIONE, MAMILLIUS, *and Ladies enter.*

HERMIONE
Take the boy. He is such a pest I can't take it anymore.

FIRST LADY
Come with me, my gracious lord. Shall I play with you?

MAMILLIUS
No, I don't want anything to do with you.

FIRST LADY
Why, my sweet lord?

MAMILLIUS
You'll kiss me too hard and talk baby talk to me. (*to Second Lady*) I love you better.

SECOND LADY
Why is that, my lord?

MAMILLIUS
Not because your eyebrows are blacker, though they say that black eyebrows suit some women best, as long as there isn't too much hair and they are shaped like a semicircle, or drawn like a half-moon.

SECOND LADY
Who taught you that?

MAMILLIUS
I learned it from looking at women's faces. Tell me, what color are your eyebrows?

FIRST LADY
Blue, my lord.

MAMILLIUS

    Nay, that's a mock: I have seen a lady's nose

20   That has been blue, but not her eyebrows.

FIRST LADY

                            Hark ye;

    The queen your mother rounds apace: we shall

    Present our services to a fine new prince

    One of these days; and then you'd wanton with us,

25   If we would have you.

SECOND LADY

                 She is spread of late

    Into a goodly bulk: good time encounter her!

HERMIONE

    What wisdom stirs amongst you? Come, sir, now

    I am for you again: pray you, sit by us,

30   And tell 's a tale.

MAMILLIUS

            Merry or sad shall 't be?

HERMIONE

    As merry as you will.

MAMILLIUS

    A sad tale's best for winter: I have one

    Of sprites and goblins.

HERMIONE

35   Let's have that, good sir.

    Come on, sit down: come on, and do your best

    To fright me with your sprites; you're powerful at it.

MAMILLIUS

    There was a man—

HERMIONE

             Nay, come, sit down; then on.

MAMILLIUS

40   Dwelt by a churchyard: I will tell it softly;

    Yond crickets shall not hear it.

HERMIONE

              Come on, then,

    And give 't me in mine ear.

MAMILLUS

No, you're joking. I've seen a lady's nose that was blue, but not her eyebrows.

FIRST LADY

Listen: Your mother the queen is getting rounder by the day. We'll be serving a fine new prince one day soon, and then you'll want to play with us, if we'll let you.

SECOND LADY

She has become quite big lately. May it come quickly for her!

HERMIONE

What are you talking about now? Come, sir, now I'm ready for you again. Sit next to me, and tell me a story.

MAMILLIUS

Should it be happy or sad?

HERMIONE

As happy as you'd like.

MAMILLIUS

A sad story is best for the winter. I have one about fairies and goblins.

HERMIONE

Let's hear it, good sir. Come on, sit down, and try to frighten me with your fairies. You're good at it.

MAMILLIUS

There was a man—

HERMIONE

No, sit down, and then tell me.

MAMILLIUS

—who lived by a churchyard. I'll tell it quietly, so those other ladies won't hear it.

HERMIONE

Come on then, and tell me in my ear.

Enter LEONTES, *with* ANTIGONUS, LORDS, *and others*

LEONTES
Was he met there? his train? Camillo with him?

FIRST LORD
45 Behind the tuft of pines I met them; never
Saw I men scour so on their way: I eyed them
Even to their ships.

LEONTES
How blest am I
In my just censure, in my true opinion!
50 Alack, for lesser knowledge! how accursed
In being so blest! There may be in the cup
A spider steep'd, and one may drink, depart,
And yet partake no venom, for his knowledge
Is not infected: but if one present
55 The abhorr'd ingredient to his eye, make known
How he hath drunk, he cracks his gorge, his sides,
With violent hefts. I have drunk, and seen the spider.
Camillo was his help in this, his pander:
There is a plot against my life, my crown;
60 All's true that is mistrusted: that false villain
Whom I employ'd was pre-employ'd by him:
He has discover'd my design, and I
Remain a pinch'd thing; yea, a very trick
For them to play at will. How came the posterns
65 So easily open?

FIRST LORD
By his great authority;
Which often hath no less prevail'd than so
On your command.

LEONTES
I know 't too well.
70 Give me the boy: I am glad you did not nurse him:
Though he does bear some signs of me, yet you
Have too much blood in him.

LEONTES, ANTIGONUS, LORDS, *and others enter.*

LEONTES

Did his men meet him there? Camillo was with him?

FIRST LORD

I ran across them behind the pine grove. I've never seen men move so quickly along. I saw them go all the way to their ships.

LEONTES

I'm so blessed to have such accurate judgment, and such a correct opinion! Alas, if only I knew less! I'm cursed to be so blessed! There may be a spider in your cup, and if you drink without realizing it, you aren't hurt. But if you see the spider and know you have drunk it, you will wretch and heave violently. I have drunk from the cup, and I know that the spider was in it. Camillo helped him and acted as his pimp. There is a plot to kill me and take my place as king. Everything that I suspected is true. That traitorous villain I employed actually worked for Polixenes. He has discovered my plan, and I'm still tormented, a toy for them to play with. How were the gates so easily opened?

FIRST LORD

By Camillo's authority, which he's often wielded by your command.

LEONTES

I know it too well. Give me the boy. I am glad you didn't breastfeed him. He may look a bit like me, but he looks too much like you.

HERMIONE

What is this? sport?

LEONTES

Bear the boy hence; he shall not come about her;
75   Away with him! and let her sport herself
With that she's big with; for 'tis Polixenes
Has made thee swell thus.

HERMIONE

But I'd say he had not,
And I'll be sworn you would believe my saying,
80   Howe'er you lean to the nayward.

LEONTES

You, my lords,
Look on her, mark her well; be but about
To say 'she is a goodly lady,' and
The justice of your hearts will thereto add
85   ''Tis pity she's not honest, honourable:'
Praise her but for this her without-door form,
Which on my faith deserves high speech, and straight
The shrug, the hum or ha, these petty brands
That calumny doth use—O, I am out—
90   That mercy does, for calumny will sear
Virtue itself: these shrugs, these hums and ha's,
When you have said 'she's goodly,' come between
Ere you can say 'she's honest:' but be 't known,
From him that has most cause to grieve it should be,
95   She's an adulteress.

HERMIONE

Should a villain say so,
The most replenish'd villain in the world,
He were as much more villain: you, my lord,
Do but mistake.

LEONTES

You have mistook, my lady,
100   Polixenes for Leontes: O thou thing!
Which I'll not call a creature of thy place,

HERMIONE

What is this? A joke?

LEONTES

Take the boy away. He won't be near her anymore. Take him away! Let her play with the one she's pregnant with now, since it is Polixenes's child.

HERMIONE

I'll say it is not and will swear that you should believe me, whatever you think to the contrary.

LEONTES

My lords, look at her closely. If you are tempted to say, "She is a fine lady," the wisdom of your hearts will add, "A shame that she isn't virtuous or honorable." Praise her for anything but her outward form, which does deserve praise, and immediately you must shrug or mutter to yourself. Those are the expressions that slander uses—no, I'm wrong—that mercy uses, because slander only attacks someone who is virtuous. These shrugs and mutterings after you say, "She's goodly" interrupt you before you can say, "She's virtuous." Listen to the man who has the most reason to be upset about it: she's an adulteress.

HERMIONE

If a villain said so, the worst in the world, saying so would make him even more of a villain. My lord, you are mistaken.

LEONTES

My lady, you have mistaken Polixenes for me. Oh, you creature! I won't give you the title that goes with your high social status, or I'll set a precedent allowing rudeness

Lest barbarism, making me the precedent,
Should a like language use to all degrees
105 And mannerly distinguishment leave out
Betwixt the prince and beggar: I have said
She's an adulteress; I have said with whom:
More, she's a traitor and Camillo is
A federary with her, and one that knows
110 What she should shame to know herself
But with her most vile principal, that she's
A bed-swerver, even as bad as those
That vulgars give bold'st titles, ay, and privy
To this their late escape.

HERMIONE
115   No, by my life.
Privy to none of this. How will this grieve you,
When you shall come to clearer knowledge, that
You thus have publish'd me! Gentle my lord,
You scarce can right me throughly then to say
120 You did mistake.

LEONTES
                                No; if I mistake
In those foundations which I build upon,
The centre is not big enough to bear
A school-boy's top. Away with her! to prison!
125 He who shall speak for her is afar off guilty
But that he speaks.

HERMIONE
                              There's some ill planet reigns:
I must be patient till the heavens look
With an aspect more favourable. Good my lords,
130 I am not prone to weeping, as our sex
Commonly are; the want of which vain dew
Perchance shall dry your pities: but I have
That honourable grief lodged here which burns
Worse than tears drown: beseech you all, my lords,
135 With thoughts so qualified as your charities

to use the same names for everyone and not distinguish between a prince and a beggar. I have said she is an adulteress, and I have said with whom. Even more than that, she is a traitor, and she is in league with Camillo, who knows what she should be ashamed of: that she's an adulteress. She's as bad as the women that common people give the coarsest name to, and she knew that they were escaping.

HERMIONE

No, I swear on my life I knew none of this. You'll regret publicly shaming me like this when you realize you are wrong! My gentle lord, you can make it all right again by saying you made a mistake.

LEONTES

No. If I am wrong about this, then the Earth isn't big enough to hold a schoolboy's **top**. Take her to prison! Anyone who would defend her is indirectly as guilty as she is, just by speaking.

A top for spinning, such as schoolboys would play with.

HERMIONE

The stars must be aligned in a way that is making everyone mad! I must be patient until their positions change. My good lords, I don't cry as much as other women do, which might make you think I'm not deserving of pity. But my honorable grief burns more fiercely than tears can extinguish. I beg you all, my lords, judge me in as measured a manner as your sense of charity will allow. And so carry out the king's will!

Shall best instruct you, measure me; and so
The king's will be perform'd!

LEONTES

Shall I be heard?

HERMIONE

Who is 't that goes with me? Beseech your highness,
140   My women may be with me; for you see
My plight requires it. Do not weep, good fools;
There is no cause: when you shall know your mistress
Has deserved prison, then abound in tears
As I come out: this action I now go on
145   Is for my better grace. Adieu, my lord:
I never wish'd to see you sorry; now
I trust I shall. My women, come; you have leave.

LEONTES

Go, do our bidding; hence!

Exeunt HERMIONE, *guarded; with Ladies*

FIRST LORD

Beseech your highness, call the queen again.

ANTIGONUS

150   Be certain what you do, sir, lest your justice
Prove violence; in the which three great ones suffer,
Yourself, your queen, your son.

FIRST LORD

For her, my lord,
I dare my life lay down and will do 't, sir,
155   Please you to accept it, that the queen is spotless
I' the eyes of heaven and to you; I mean,
In this which you accuse her.

ANTIGONUS

If it prove
She's otherwise, I'll keep my stables where
160   I lodge my wife; I'll go in couples with her;
Than when I feel and see her no farther trust her;
For every inch of woman in the world,

LEONTES

Will I be obeyed?

HERMIONE

Who will go with me? Your highness, I beg that my
women might go with me, since I need help in my
condition. Don't cry, my dear ones. There's no reason to.
If you ever know that your mistress is guilty and deserves
to be in prison, then you can cry when I come out. But
since I'm innocent, this trial I'm enduring will make me
more virtuous. Goodbye, my lord. I never wanted to see
you feeling sorry, but now I know I will. My women,
come, you have permission.

LEONTES

Go on, do as I say!

HERMIONE and her Ladies exit, surrounded by guards.

FIRST LORD

Your highness, I beg you, call the queen back.

ANTIGONUS

Be sure of what you are doing, sir, or what you think
is justice might prove to be injustice, and three great
people might suffer—you, your queen, and your son.

FIRST LORD

My lord, I would lay down my life for the queen in
belief that she is virtuous in both the eyes of heaven
and to you. She is innocent of what you accuse her of.

*Scholars have
generally
interpreted
Shakespeare's
original passage
in two different
ways: The first is
the version given
here; the second
is that Antigonus
means he will
treat his wife's
lodgings as he
treats his stables,
where mares
and stallions
are kept apart.*

ANTIGONUS

If it turns out she's unfaithful, **I'll guard my wife as** ←
vigilantly as I guard my horses, and I'll go about
leashed together with her. I will only trust her when I can
touch her or see her, because if the queen is lying, then
every woman in the world must be a liar.

Ay, every dram of woman's flesh is false,
If she be.

LEONTES

165   Hold your peaces.

FIRST LORD

                              Good my lord,—

ANTIGONUS

It is for you we speak, not for ourselves:
You are abused and by some putter-on
That will be damn'd for 't; would I knew the villain,
170 I would land-damn him. Be she honour-flaw'd,
I have three daughters; the eldest is eleven
The second and the third, nine, and some five;
If this prove true, they'll pay for 't: by mine honour,
I'll geld 'em all; fourteen they shall not see,
175 To bring false generations: they are co-heirs;
And I had rather glib myself than they
Should not produce fair issue.

LEONTES

                              Cease; no more.
You smell this business with a sense as cold
180 As is a dead man's nose: but I do see 't and feel 't
As you feel doing thus; and see withal
The instruments that feel.

ANTIGONUS

                              If it be so,
We need no grave to bury honesty:
185 There's not a grain of it the face to sweeten
Of the whole dungy earth.

LEONTES

                              What! lack I credit?

FIRST LORD

I had rather you did lack than I, my lord,
Upon this ground; and more it would content me
190 To have her honour true than your suspicion,
Be blamed for 't how you might.

LEONTES

> Be quiet.

FIRST LORD

> My good lord—

ANTIGONUS

> We're speaking for your sake, not our own. Some liar has abused your confidence, and he'll be damned for it. If I knew who it was, I would thrash him without pity. If the queen isn't honorable, my three daughters will pay for it, by my honor. The oldest is eleven, the next is nine, and the third is about five, and I'll make them all incapable of bearing children. They'll be unable to have illegitimate children by the time they're fourteen. They are all my heirs, and I'd rather castrate myself than have them bear anything other than legitimate children.

LEONTES

> Stop. Say no more. You're about as perceptive as a dead man, but I see it and feel it **as you feel this.** And I also see the fingers that feel.

Leontes likely performs some action, such as touching an object, to demonstrate.

ANTIGONUS

> If it is true, we don't need a grave to bury honesty, because it means that there is not a shred of it on this earth.

LEONTES

> What? You don't believe me?

FIRST LORD

> My lord, I would rather you be wrong than me in this instance. And I'd rather it turn out that she is honorable than that you are right, regardless of how you're blamed for it.

LEONTES

                     Why, what need we
Commune with you of this, but rather follow
Our forceful instigation? Our prerogative
195   Calls not your counsels, but our natural goodness
Imparts this; which if you, or stupefied
Or seeming so in skill, cannot or will not
Relish a truth like us, inform yourselves
We need no more of your advice: the matter,
200   The loss, the gain, the ordering on 't, is all
Properly ours.

ANTIGONUS

              And I wish, my liege,
You had only in your silent judgment tried it,
Without more overture.

LEONTES

205   How could that be?
Either thou art most ignorant by age,
Or thou wert born a fool. Camillo's flight,
Added to their familiarity,
Which was as gross as ever touch'd conjecture,
210   That lack'd sight only, nought for approbation
But only seeing, all other circumstances
Made up to the deed, doth push on this proceeding:
Yet, for a greater confirmation,
For in an act of this importance 'twere
215   Most piteous to be wild, I have dispatch'd in post
To sacred Delphos, to Apollo's temple,
Cleomenes and Dion, whom you know
Of stuff'd sufficiency: now from the oracle
They will bring all; whose spiritual counsel had,
220   Shall stop or spur me. Have I done well?

FIRST LORD

                  Well done, my lord.

LEONTES

> Why do I have to debate this with you, instead of just
> following my own strong impulse? As king I'm not
> required to seek your advice, though I tell you this
> information out of natural goodness. But if you, who are
> either confused or pretend to be, can't understand the
> truth as I do, then I don't need any more of your advice.
> The entire affair is in my hands.

ANTIGONUS

> My lord, I only wish you had spent more time
> considering your judgment, without making it public.

LEONTES

> How do you mean? Either you have become a fool with
> age, or you were born that way. Camillo's fleeing and
> their intimacy, which was as obvious as any suspicion that
> lacked only an eyewitness to confirm it, together push
> this matter forward. Still, since this is a serious matter
> and shouldn't be handled rashly, I've sent Cleomenes
> and Dion to get further confirmation at Apollo's temple
> in Delphos. You know they are competent. They'll bring
> word from the oracle, and I'll heed whatever advice it
> gives, whether for or against my suspicion. Is that good?

FIRST LORD

> Very good, my lord.

LEONTES
Though I am satisfied and need no more
Than what I know, yet shall the oracle
Give rest to the minds of others, such as he
225   Whose ignorant credulity will not
Come up to the truth. So have we thought it good
From our free person she should be confined,
Lest that the treachery of the two fled hence
Be left her to perform. Come, follow us;
230   We are to speak in public; for this business
Will raise us all.

ANTIGONUS
(*aside*)   To laughter, as I take it,
If the good truth were known.

Exeunt

LEONTES

> Even though I am sure that I am right, the oracle
> will convince everyone else, such as those who find
> themselves unable to accept the truth. So I have thought
> it a good idea to confine her and keep her away from me,
> so the treachery of Camillo and Polixenes is not left to her
> to perform. Come, follow me. I'm going to speak to the
> public, since this matter will incite everyone to action.

ANTIGONUS

> (*aside*) Incite everyone to laughter, I believe, if the truth
> were known.

> *They all exit.*

ACT 2, SCENE 2

A prison.
Enter PAULINA, *a Gentleman, and Attendants*

PAULINA

The keeper of the prison, call to him;
let him have knowledge who I am.

Exit Gentleman

Good lady,
No court in Europe is too good for thee;
5   What dost thou then in prison?

Re-enter Gentleman, with the GAOLER

Now, good sir,
You know me, do you not?

GAOLER

For a worthy lady
And one whom much I honour.

PAULINA

10   Pray you then,
Conduct me to the queen.

GAOLER

I may not, madam:
To the contrary I have express commandment.

PAULINA

Here's ado, to lock up honesty and honour from
15   The access of gentle visitors! Is 't lawful, pray you,
To see her women? any of them? Emilia?

GAOLER

So please you, madam,
To put apart these your attendants, I
Shall bring Emilia forth.

ACT 2, SCENE 2

A prison.
PAULINA, *a Gentleman, and Attendants enter.*

PAULINA

Call the prison overseer. Tell him who I am.

The Gentleman exits.

No court in Europe is good enough for you, good lady, so why are you in prison?

The gentleman re-enters, with the JAILER.

Good sir, you know me, don't you?

JAILER

I know you as a worthy woman and one I have great respect for.

PAULINA

Please, then, take me to the queen.

JAILER

I can't, madam. I have explicit orders not to.

PAULINA

Such a fuss just to keep kind visitors from seeing such an honest and honorable lady! Am I allowed to see her attendants? Any of them? Emilia?

JAILER

If you would please send away your attendants, I'll bring out Emilia.

PAULINA

20   I pray now, call her.
Withdraw yourselves.

Exeunt Gentleman and Attendants

GAOLER
And, madam, I must be present at your conference.
PAULINA
Well, be 't so, prithee.

Exit GAOLER

Here's such ado to make no stain a stain
25   As passes colouring.

Re-enter GAOLER, *with* EMILIA

Dear gentlewoman,
How fares our gracious lady?
EMILIA
As well as one so great and so forlorn
May hold together: on her frights and griefs,
30   Which never tender lady hath born greater,
She is something before her time deliver'd.
PAULINA
A boy?
EMILIA
A daughter, and a goodly babe,
Lusty and like to live: the queen receives
35   Much comfort in 't; says 'My poor prisoner,
I am innocent as you.'
PAULINA
I dare be sworn
These dangerous unsafe lunes i' the king, beshrew them!
He must be told on 't, and he shall: the office
40   Becomes a woman best; I'll take 't upon me:
If I prove honey-mouth'd let my tongue blister

PAULINA

> Please, call her. (*to her attendants*) Leave me here.
> > *The Gentleman and the Attendants exit.*

JAILER

> Madam, I must be present while you speak with Emilia.

PAULINA

> Well, if you must.

> > *The* JAILER *exits.*

> What a great effort to make the queen guilty beyond
> justification when she is actually innocent.

> *The* JAILER *re-enters with* EMILIA.

> Dear gentlewoman, how is our gracious lady?

EMILIA

> As well as can be expected for one so great and so sad.
> Because of her overwhelming grief and fright, which are
> greater than a kind woman has ever suffered, she has
> delivered her baby prematurely.

PAULINA

> A boy?

EMILIA

> A strong and healthy daughter. The queen draws comfort
> from the child, saying, "My poor prisoner, I am as
> innocent as you are."

PAULINA

> I swear that the king must give up these dangerous fits
> of madness—curse them! He must be told, and I'll do
> it—it's a task best suited to a woman. If I am deceitful,
> let my tongue blister and never be capable of expressing
> my anger ever again. Please, Emilia, tell the queen that

And never to my red-look'd anger be
The trumpet any more. Pray you, Emilia,
Commend my best obedience to the queen:
45   If she dares trust me with her little babe,
I'll show 't the king and undertake to be
Her advocate to the loud'st. We do not know
How he may soften at the sight o' the child:
The silence often of pure innocence
50   Persuades when speaking fails.

EMILIA

                              Most worthy madam,
Your honour and your goodness is so evident
That your free undertaking cannot miss
A thriving issue: there is no lady living
55   So meet for this great errand. Please your ladyship
To visit the next room, I'll presently
Acquaint the queen of your most noble offer;
Who but to-day hammer'd of this design,
But durst not tempt a minister of honour,
60   Lest she should be denied.

PAULINA

                              Tell her, Emilia.
I'll use that tongue I have: if wit flow from 't
As boldness from my bosom, let 't not be doubted
I shall do good.

EMILIA

65   Now be you blest for it!
I'll to the queen: please you,
come something nearer.

GAOLER

Madam, if 't please the queen to send the babe,
I know not what I shall incur to pass it,
70   Having no warrant.

I am her devoted supporter, and if she'll trust me with
the baby I'll show her to the king and be her loudest
advocate. Maybe he will soften up at the sight of the
child. Pure silent innocence can sometimes convince
when speech fails to do so.

EMILIA

Worthy madam, you are so obviously honorable and
good that your generous mission cannot fail to have a
positive outcome. There is no lady living more suitable
for this great errand. If you'll make your way to the next
room, I'll tell the queen of your noble offer. Just today
she had come up with a similar plan, but was afraid to
approach any noble person, fearing she'd be rejected.

PAULINA

Emilia, tell her that I'll speak as well as I can. If I have as
much intelligence as I have courage, don't doubt that I'll
do some good.

EMILIA

Bless you for it! I'll go to the queen. Please, come closer.

JAILER

Madam, if the queen wants to send the baby, I don't
know how I'll be punished for allowing it, since I don't
have any official approval.

PAULINA

                You need not fear it, sir:
This child was prisoner to the womb and is
By law and process of great nature thence
Freed and enfranchised, not a party to
75   The anger of the king nor guilty of,
If any be, the trespass of the queen.

GAOLER

I do believe it.

PAULINA

Do not you fear: upon mine honour,
I will stand betwixt you and danger.

Exeunt

PAULINA

> Don't worry, sir. The child was a prisoner of the womb, and now by natural law she is free from it. She's not part of the king's anger, or guilty of any trespass of the queen, if any even exists.

JAILER

> I believe it.

PAULINA

> Don't worry. On my honor, I will you defend you myself.

> > *They exit.*

ACT 2, SCENE 3

A room in LEONTES' *palace.*
Enter LEONTES, ANTIGONUS, LORDS, *and* SERVANTS

LEONTES

Nor night nor day no rest: it is but weakness
To bear the matter thus; mere weakness. If
The cause were not in being,—part o' the cause,
She the adulteress; for the harlot king
5   Is quite beyond mine arm, out of the blank
And level of my brain, plot-proof; but she
I can hook to me: say that she were gone,
Given to the fire, a moiety of my rest
Might come to me again. Who's there?

FIRST SERVANT

10   My lord?

LEONTES

How does the boy?

FIRST SERVANT

He took good rest to-night;
'Tis hoped his sickness is discharged.

LEONTES

                            To see his nobleness!
15   Conceiving the dishonour of his mother,
He straight declined, droop'd, took it deeply,
Fasten'd and fix'd the shame on 't in himself,
Threw off his spirit, his appetite, his sleep,
And downright languish'd. Leave me solely: go,
20   See how he fares.

                           Exit SERVANT

                Fie, fie! no thought of him:
The thought of my revenges that way
Recoil upon me: in himself too mighty,
And in his parties, his alliance; let him be

ACT 2, SCENE 3

A room in LEONTES*'s palace.*

LEONTES, ANTIGONUS, LORDS, *and* SERVANTS *enter.*

LEONTES

I can't rest night or day. It is a kind of weakness to be so affected by this issue. If only the cause of it were no longer alive—part of the cause, at least, the adulteress. The lecherous king is away from here, which puts him beyond my aim and anything I could do to him. But she, the adulteress, I can keep close. If she were **burned at the stake**, perhaps I would have some small bit of rest. Who's there?

> *A punishment for treason against the king.*

FIRST SERVANT

My lord?

LEONTES

How is the boy doing?

FIRST SERVANT

He slept well tonight, and we hope that he's gotten over his illness.

LEONTES

I'm amazed at his nobility! Recognizing the dishonorable behavior of his mother, he immediately began to decline, to feel the shame himself. He became sad, stopped eating, stopped sleeping, and grew weak. Leave me alone, and go see how he's doing.

The SERVANT *exits.*

No! I won't think about Polixenes. I fear taking revenge on him. He himself is too powerful, and he has powerful allies. Let him be until an opportunity comes. I'll have revenge now on her. Camillo and Polixenes laugh at me

25 Until a time may serve: for present vengeance,
Take it on her. Camillo and Polixenes
Laugh at me, make their pastime at my sorrow:
They should not laugh if I could reach them, nor
Shall she within my power.

Enter PAULINA, *with a child*

FIRST LORD
30   You must not enter.
PAULINA
Nay, rather, good my lords, be second to me:
Fear you his tyrannous passion more, alas,
Than the queen's life? a gracious innocent soul,
More free than he is jealous.
ANTIGONUS
35   That's enough.
SECOND SERVANT
Madam, he hath not slept tonight; commanded
None should come at him.
PAULINA
                        Not so hot, good sir:
I come to bring him sleep. 'Tis such as you,
40 That creep like shadows by him and do sigh
At each his needless heavings, such as you
Nourish the cause of his awaking: I
Do come with words as medicinal as true,
Honest as either, to purge him of that humour
45 That presses him from sleep.
LEONTES
                        What noise there, ho?
PAULINA
No noise, my lord; but needful conference
About some gossips for your highness.

and find amusement in my sorrow. They wouldn't laugh if I could reach them, and neither will the woman who is within my power to punish.

PAULINA *enters with a child.*

FIRST LORD

You must not go in.

PAULINA

No, my good lords, back me. Do you fear his tyrannical anger more than the queen's life? She's a gracious, innocent soul, more innocent than he is jealous.

ANTIGONUS

That's enough.

SECOND SERVANT

Madam, he hasn't slept tonight and has ordered that he be left alone.

PAULINA

Not so hasty, good sir. I'm here to bring him sleep. It's people like you who creep softly around him like shadows and sigh at his unnecessary agitation that feed the cause of his wakefulness. I have something to say to him that's as soothing as it is true, and honest as well, that will rid him of the sickness keeping him from rest.

LEONTES

What is that noise?

PAULINA

It's not noise, my lord, but necessary talk about godparents for your highness.

LEONTES

How!

50   Away with that audacious lady! Antigonus,
I charged thee that she should not come about me:
I knew she would.

ANTIGONUS

I told her so, my lord,
On your displeasure's peril and on mine,
55   She should not visit you.

LEONTES

What, canst not rule her?

PAULINA

From all dishonesty he can: in this,
Unless he take the course that you have done,
Commit me for committing honour, trust it,
60   He shall not rule me.

ANTIGONUS

La you now, you hear:
When she will take the rein I let her run;
But she'll not stumble.

PAULINA

Good my liege, I come;
65   And, I beseech you, hear me, who profess
Myself your loyal servant, your physician,
Your most obedient counsellor, yet that dare
Less appear so in comforting your evils,
Than such as most seem yours: I say, I come
70   From your good queen.

LEONTES

Good queen!

PAULINA

Good queen, my lord,
Good queen; I say good queen;
And would by combat make her good, so were I
75   A man, the worst about you.

LEONTES

> What! Take this bold woman away! Antigonus, I told you to keep her away from me, because I knew she would come.

ANTIGONUS

> My lord, I told her that she shouldn't visit you, or she'd risk making us both angry.

LEONTES

> What, you can't control her?

PAULINA

> He can keep me from dishonesty. Unless he does as you've done and locks me up for being honorable, he won't control me in this matter.

ANTIGONUS

> You see, when she wants to take control I give her room, but she'll do what's right.

PAULINA

> My good lord, I beg you to listen to me. I'm your loyal servant, your doctor, your most obedient adviser, though perhaps I don't seem like it because I won't condone your evil actions, as do those servants who only seem most loyal. I come from your good queen.

LEONTES

> Good queen!

PAULINA

> She is a good queen, my lord. I say she is a good queen, a very good queen. If I were a man I would fight a duel to prove her innocence, even against the most lowly man.

LEONTES

Force her hence.

PAULINA

Let him that makes but trifles of his eyes
First hand me: on mine own accord I'll off;
But first I'll do my errand. The good queen,
80 For she is good, hath brought you forth a daughter;
Here 'tis; commends it to your blessing.

Laying down the child

LEONTES

Out!

A mankind witch! Hence with her, out o' door:
A most intelligencing bawd!

PAULINA

85 Not so:

I am as ignorant in that as you
In so entitling me, and no less honest
Than you are mad; which is enough, I'll warrant,
As this world goes, to pass for honest.

LEONTES

90 Traitors!

Will you not push her out? Give her the bastard.
Thou dotard! thou art woman-tired, unroosted
By thy dame Partlet here. Take up the bastard;
Take 't up, I say; give 't to thy crone.

PAULINA

95 For ever

Unvenerable be thy hands, if thou
Takest up the princess by that forced baseness
Which he has put upon 't!

LEONTES

He dreads his wife.

PAULINA

100 So I would you did; then 'twere past all doubt
You'd call your children yours.

LEONTES

Force her out of here.

PAULINA

The first man who tries to manhandle me better not value his eyes. I'll go by my own accord, but first I'll carry out my errand. The good queen, for she is good, has given birth to a daughter. Here she is. She commends her to you so that you may bless her.

She lays the child down.

LEONTES

Get out! This furious witch! Take her out of here! She's a spying pimp!

PAULINA

Not at all. I know nothing about that, while you show your knowledge of it by calling me that name. I'm as honest as you are mad, which, I assure you, is as honest as you can expect in this world.

LEONTES

Traitors! Won't you shove her out? Hand her the bastard child! You dolt! You are hen-pecked and kicked out of your place of authority by your hen here. Pick up that bastard. Pick it up, I say, and give it to your hag.

PAULINA

(*to Antigonus*) Your hands will forever be unworthy of respect if you take up the princess under that terrible name he called her!

LEONTES

He fears his wife.

PAULINA

I wish you did, too, and then you would undoubtedly call your children your own.

LEONTES

A nest of traitors!

ANTIGONUS

I am none, by this good light.

PAULINA

Nor I, nor any
105 But one that's here, and that's himself, for he
The sacred honour of himself, his queen's,
His hopeful son's, his babe's, betrays to slander,
Whose sting is sharper than the sword's; and will not—
For, as the case now stands, it is a curse
110 He cannot be compell'd to 't—once remove
The root of his opinion, which is rotten
As ever oak or stone was sound.

LEONTES

A callat
Of boundless tongue, who late hath beat her husband
115 And now baits me! This brat is none of mine;
It is the issue of Polixenes:
Hence with it, and together with the dam
Commit them to the fire!

PAULINA

It is yours;
120 And, might we lay the old proverb to your charge,
So like you, 'tis the worse. Behold, my lords,
Although the print be little, the whole matter
And copy of the father, eye, nose, lip,
The trick of 's frown, his forehead, nay, the valley,
125 The pretty dimples of his chin and cheek, his smiles,
The very mould and frame of hand, nail, finger:
And thou, good goddess Nature, which hast made it
So like to him that got it, if thou hast
The ordering of the mind too, 'mongst all colours
130 No yellow in 't, lest she suspect, as he does,
Her children not her husband's!

LEONTES

> A nest of traitors!

ANTIGONUS

> I'm not one.

PAULINA

> Nor am I, nor is anyone else here other than himself, since he has betrayed his own honor, the honor of his wife, of his son, and of his baby with slander, which is sharper than any sword. It's a curse that he can't be forced to revise his opinion, which is as rotten as oak or stone is solid.

LEONTES

> A constantly chattering harlot, who has recently beat her husband and now provokes me. This brat isn't mine—it's Polixenes's child. Take it away, and send it and its mother to the fire!

PAULINA

> It is yours. It looks so much like you, and for the worse, as the proverb puts it. See, my lords, how the baby has all the features of her father in miniature: the eyes, nose, lips, her father's frown and forehead, the dimples on his chin and cheeks, his smile. They have the same hands, nails, fingers. And so good goddess Nature has made the baby just like the man who conceived her. If Nature has control over temperament, too, don't let her have any jealousy, or she'll suspect, as her father does, that her children are not her husband's!

LEONTES
                                        A gross hag
And, lozel, thou art worthy to be hang'd,
That wilt not stay her tongue.

ANTIGONUS
                                        Hang all the husbands
135   That cannot do that feat, you'll leave yourself
Hardly one subject.

LEONTES
                              Once more, take her hence.

PAULINA
A most unworthy and unnatural lord
140   Can do no more.

LEONTES
                    I'll ha' thee burnt.

PAULINA
                                        I care not:
It is an heretic that makes the fire,
Not she which burns in 't. I'll not call you tyrant;
145   But this most cruel usage of your queen,
Not able to produce more accusation
Than your own weak-hinged fancy, something savours
Of tyranny and will ignoble make you,
Yea, scandalous to the world.

LEONTES
                                        On your allegiance,
150   Out of the chamber with her! Were I a tyrant,
Where were her life? she durst not call me so,
If she did know me one. Away with her!

PAULINA
I pray you, do not push me; I'll be gone.
155   Look to your babe, my lord; 'tis yours: Jove send her
A better guiding spirit! What needs these hands?
You, that are thus so tender o'er his follies,
Will never do him good, not one of you.
So, so: farewell; we are gone.

                                                    Exit

NO FEAR SHAKESPEARE

LEONTES

> (*to Antigonus*) A horrible woman. Scoundrel, you ought to be hanged for not stopping her from speaking.

ANTIGONUS

> If you hang all the husbands who can't keep their wives from talking, you'll have hardly any subjects left.

LEONTES

> Once again, get her out of here.

PAULINA

> A most unworthy and unnatural lord can do only that.

LEONTES

> I'll have you burnt.

PAULINA

> I don't care. It would be a heretic building the fire, not the woman burning in it. I won't call you a tyrant, but your cruel mistreatment of your queen seems something like tyranny, since you can't produce any evidence beyond your own weak imaginings. It will make you dishonorable, even scandalous, to all the world.

LEONTES

> Be loyal to me and take her out of the room! If I were a tyrant, would she still be alive? If she knew I was a tyrant, truly, she wouldn't dare call me one. Take her away!

PAULINA

> Please don't push me. I'll go. Look at your baby, my lord. She's yours. May Jove send her a better protector! (*to attendants*) Why do you put your hands on me? All of you who are so accepting of his misbehavior won't do him any good, not one of you. So, goodbye, I'm going.

> *She exits.*

LEONTES

160   Thou, traitor, hast set on thy wife to this.
     My child? away with 't! Even thou, that hast
     A heart so tender o'er it, take it hence
     And see it instantly consumed with fire;
     Even thou and none but thou. Take it up straight:
165   Within this hour bring me word 'tis done,
     And by good testimony, or I'll seize thy life,
     With what thou else call'st thine. If thou refuse
     And wilt encounter with my wrath, say so;
     The bastard brains with these my proper hands
170   Shall I dash out. Go, take it to the fire;
     For thou set'st on thy wife.

ANTIGONUS

                      I did not, sir:
     These lords, my noble fellows, if they please,
     Can clear me in 't.

LORDS

175   We can: my royal liege,
     He is not guilty of her coming hither.

LEONTES

     You're liars all.

FIRST LORD

     Beseech your highness, give us better credit:
     We have always truly served you, and beseech you
180   So to esteem of us, and on our knees we beg,
     As recompense of our dear services
     Past and to come, that you do change this purpose,
     Which being so horrible, so bloody, must
     Lead on to some foul issue: we all kneel.

LEONTES

185   I am a feather for each wind that blows:
     Shall I live on to see this bastard kneel
     And call me father? better burn it now
     Than curse it then. But be it; let it live.
     It shall not neither. You, sir, come you hither;

LEONTES

(*to Antigonus*) You traitor! You put your wife up to this.
My child? Get rid of it! You, who have such a tender heart
for it, take it away and see that it's burned immediately.
You, and no one but you. Do it now. Within the hour I
want to hear that it is done, and with witnesses, or I'll
have your life, and all else that you call your own. If
you refuse and will face my anger, say so. I'll dash the
bastard's brains out with my own hands. Go, take it to the
fire, since you put your wife up to this.

ANTIGONUS

I didn't, sir. These lords, my noble fellows, will clear
my name.

LORDS

We can, my royal lord. He isn't responsible for her
appearance here.

LEONTES

You are all liars.

FIRST LORD

Please, your highness, we are more honorable than
that. We have always served you faithfully and beg you
to think of us that way. We beg you on our knees, as
repayment for all our services of the past and future, that
you'll change your mind. This plan is so horrible and
bloody that it can only lead to something terrible.

LEONTES

I am asked to follow every opinion I hear. Should I allow
this bastard to grow up and call me father? I'd rather
burn it now than curse it then. But, fine, let it live. (*to
Antigonus*) You, sir, come here. You have interfered
so kindly along with your wench in order to save this

190   You that have been so tenderly officious
    With Lady Margery, your midwife there,
    To save this bastard's life,—for 'tis a bastard,
    So sure as this beard's grey, —what will you adventure
    To save this brat's life?

ANTIGONUS

195   Any thing, my lord,
    That my ability may undergo
    And nobleness impose: at least thus much:
    I'll pawn the little blood which I have left
    To save the innocent: any thing possible.

LEONTES

200   It shall be possible. Swear by this sword
    Thou wilt perform my bidding.

ANTIGONUS

                            I will, my lord.

LEONTES

    Mark and perform it, see'st thou! for the fail
    Of any point in 't shall not only be
205   Death to thyself but to thy lewd-tongued wife,
    Whom for this time we pardon. We enjoin thee,
    As thou art liege-man to us, that thou carry
    This female bastard hence and that thou bear it
    To some remote and desert place quite out
210   Of our dominions, and that there thou leave it,
    Without more mercy, to its own protection
    And favour of the climate. As by strange fortune
    It came to us, I do in justice charge thee,
    On thy soul's peril and thy body's torture,
215   That thou commend it strangely to some place
    Where chance may nurse or end it. Take it up.

bastard's life—and I'm as certain it's a bastard as I am that your beard is gray—so what will you risk to save the brat's life?

ANTIGONUS

Anything that my ability will allow and that nobility would demand. I'd give what little blood I might have left to save this innocent child. I'll do whatever is possible.

LEONTES

It will be possible. Swear by this sword that you will do what I demand.

ANTIGONUS

I will, my lord.

LEONTES

Make note of what I tell you, and perform it, because if you fail to do any part of it not only will you die, but so will your crudely outspoken wife, whom I'll pardon for now. I command you, as my loyal servant, to take this female bastard away to some deserted place far from my kingdom, and to leave it there without mercy, left to its own abilities and the whims of the weather. Since it came to me because of a foreigner, it is only just that I order you, on pain of death and torture, to take it to a foreign place where luck might nurture or kill it. Pick it up.

ANTIGONUS

I swear to do this, though a present death
Had been more merciful. Come on, poor babe:
Some powerful spirit instruct the kites and ravens
220   To be thy nurses! Wolves and bears, they say
Casting their savageness aside have done
Like offices of pity. Sir, be prosperous
In more than this deed does require! And blessing
Against this cruelty fight on thy side,
225   Poor thing, condemn'd to loss!

Exit with the child

LEONTES

No, I'll not rear
Another's issue.

Enter a **SERVANT**

SERVANT

Please your highness, posts
From those you sent to the oracle are come
230   An hour since: Cleomenes and Dion,
Being well arrived from Delphos, are both landed,
Hasting to the court.

FIRST LORD

So please you, sir, their speed
Hath been beyond account.

LEONTES

Twenty-three days
235   They have been absent: 'tis good speed; foretells
The great Apollo suddenly will have
The truth of this appear. Prepare you, lords;
Summon a session, that we may arraign
240   Our most disloyal lady, for, as she hath
Been publicly accused, so shall she have
A just and open trial. While she lives
My heart will be a burthen to me. Leave me,
And think upon my bidding.

Exeunt

ANTIGONUS

I swear to carry out your orders, though killing her right now would have been more merciful. Come on, poor baby. May some powerful angel call on the vultures and ravens to take care of you. They say that wolves and bears have given up their savageness to perform similar acts of pity. Sir, be prosperous in more ways than this act deserves! (*to the baby*) And may a prayer against this cruel act help you, poor thing, condemned to die!

He exits with the child.

LEONTES

No, I won't raise another man's child.

A **SERVANT** *enters.*

SERVANT

Your highness, messages from the men you sent to the oracle arrived an hour ago. Cleomenes and Dion have both arrived safely from Delphos and are hurrying here to the court.

FIRST LORD

Their speed is astonishing.

LEONTES

They've been gone twenty-three days. Their speedy return predicts that great Apollo wants the truth of this matter revealed. Prepare yourselves, lords. Convene an open trial for this disloyal lady. Since she was publicly accused, she'll have an open and just trial. While she lives my heart is heavy. Leave me, and consider my orders.

They exit.

ACT THREE
SCENE 1

A sea-port in Sicilia.
Enter CLEOMENES *and* DION

CLEOMENES

    The climate's delicate, the air most sweet,
    Fertile the isle, the temple much surpassing
    The common praise it bears.

DION

                    I shall report,
5   For most it caught me, the celestial habits,
    Methinks I so should term them, and the reverence
    Of the grave wearers. O, the sacrifice!
    How ceremonious, solemn and unearthly
    It was i' the offering!

CLEOMENES

10   But of all, the burst
    And the ear-deafening voice o' the oracle,
    Kin to Jove's thunder, so surprised my sense.
    That I was nothing.

DION

              If the event o' the journey
15   Prove as successful to the queen,—O be 't so!—
    As it hath been to us rare, pleasant, speedy,
    The time is worth the use on 't.

CLEOMENES

                Great Apollo
    Turn all to the best! These proclamations,
20   So forcing faults upon Hermione,
    I little like.

ACT THREE
SCENE 1

A seaport in Sicilia.
CLEOMENES *and* DION *enter.*

CLEOMENES

Delphos's climate is exquisite, the air very sweet, the
island fertile, and the temple is even more beautiful than
people say.

DION

What most charmed me were the divine clothes and the
great respect held by the wise men who wore them. And
the sacrifice! The offering was so ceremonious, solemn,
and otherworldly!

CLEOMENES

Of everything, the sudden and deafening voice of the
oracle, like a clap of thunder, shocked me most and made
me feel like I was nothing.

DION

If only the outcome of the journey is as successful for the
queen as it was wonderful, pleasant, and quick for us, it
would be a worthwhile trip.

CLEOMENES

May great Apollo make all turn out well! I don't like
these claims accusing Hermione of faults.

DION
                The violent carriage of it
Will clear or end the business: when the oracle,
Thus by Apollo's great divine seal'd up,
25   Shall the contents discover, something rare
Even then will rush to knowledge. Go: fresh horses!
And gracious be the issue!

                                      Exeunt

DION

The rash way it has been conducted will either clear up
this business or end it. This judgment, sealed by Apollo's
priest, will reveal some wonderful knowledge to us once
it is open. Go, use fresh horses, and may the outcome
be good!

They exit.

ACT 3, SCENE 2

A court of Justice.
Enter LEONTES, *Lords, and* OFFICERS

LEONTES

This sessions, to our great grief we pronounce,
Even pushes 'gainst our heart: the party tried
The daughter of a king, our wife, and one
Of us too much beloved. Let us be clear'd
5   Of being tyrannous, since we so openly
Proceed in justice, which shall have due course,
Even to the guilt or the purgation.
Produce the prisoner.

OFFICER

It is his highness' pleasure that the queen
10   Appear in person here in court. Silence!

Enter HERMIONE *guarded;* PAULINA *and Ladies attending*

LEONTES

Read the indictment.

OFFICER

(*reads*) *Hermione, queen to the worthy Leontes, king
of Sicilia, thou art here accused and arraigned of high
treason, in committing adultery with Polixenes, king of*
15   *Bohemia, and conspiring with Camillo to take away the
life of our sovereign lord the king, thy royal husband: the
pretence whereof being by circumstances partly laid open,
thou, Hermione, contrary to the faith and allegiance of a
true subject, didst counsel and aid them, for their better*
20   *safety, to fly away by night.*

HERMIONE

Since what I am to say must be but that
Which contradicts my accusation and

ACT 3, SCENE 2

A courtroom.
LEONTES, LORDS, *and* OFFICERS *enter.*

LEONTES

> We call this session with great grief and heartache. The
> defendant is the daughter of a king, my wife, and one
> I have loved too much. Let me be cleared of acting like
> a tyrant, since I have been so open about this course of
> justice, whether it end in guilt or acquittal. Bring out
> the prisoner.

OFFICER

> It is the king's request that the queen appear in person in
> the courtroom. Silence!

> HERMIONE *enters, guarded.* PAULINA *and ladies come in with*
> *her.*

LEONTES

> Read the indictment.

OFFICER

> (*reads*) *Hermione, queen of the worthy Leontes, king of*
> *Sicilia, you are accused and arraigned for high treason,*
> *for committing adultery with Polixenes, king of Bohemia,*
> *and conspiring with Camillo to kill our sovereign king,*
> *your royal husband. Then, when the plot was accidentally*
> *discovered, you, Hermione, against the duty and faith of a*
> *loyal subject, advised them to flee by night for safety, and*
> *helped them to leave.*

HERMIONE

> Since what I'm going to say must contradict this
> accusation and the only testimony in my favor comes

The testimony on my part no other
But what comes from myself, it shall scarce boot me
25 To say 'not guilty:' mine integrity
Being counted falsehood, shall, as I express it,
Be so received. But thus: if powers divine
Behold our human actions, as they do,
I doubt not then but innocence shall make
30 False accusation blush and tyranny
Tremble at patience. You, my lord, best know,
Who least will seem to do so, my past life
Hath been as continent, as chaste, as true,
As I am now unhappy; which is more
35 Than history can pattern, though devised
And play'd to take spectators. For behold me
A fellow of the royal bed, which owe
A moiety of the throne a great king's daughter,
The mother to a hopeful prince, here standing
40 To prate and talk for life and honour 'fore
Who please to come and hear. For life, I prize it
As I weigh grief, which I would spare: for honour,
'Tis a derivative from me to mine,
And only that I stand for. I appeal
45 To your own conscience, sir, before Polixenes
Came to your court, how I was in your grace,
How merited to be so; since he came,
With what encounter so uncurrent I
Have strain'd to appear thus: if one jot beyond
50 The bound of honour, or in act or will
That way inclining, harden'd be the hearts
Of all that hear me, and my near'st of kin
Cry fie upon my grave!

LEONTES

                              I ne'er heard yet
55 That any of these bolder vices wanted
Less impudence to gainsay what they did
Than to perform it first.

from me, it hardly helps to say "not guilty." I'm believed
to be a liar, so whatever I say will be considered false.
But if the gods watch what we humans do, I don't doubt
that innocence will win out against false accusation and
tyranny. You, my lord, know that my past life has been
faithful, pure, and true, though you seem to know this
least of anyone. Those qualities are now matched by
my unhappiness, which is greater than history has ever
seen, even if it were created and performed to enthrall an
audience. Look at me, who has slept in the royal bed, who
owns part of the throne as the daughter of a great king,
the mother of the prince who will one day take the throne,
forced to defend my life and my honor in front of anyone
who cares to come and hear. I care as much for life as I
do for grief, which I could do without. Honor, though,
is passed down from me to my children, so I will make a
stand for that. I appeal to your conscience to remember
how you held me in good graces before Polixenes came
to court, and how I deserved to be regarded so. Since he
came to court, think of what was so unacceptable about
my behavior that I now appear on trial. If I have acted in
any way dishonorably, or even seemed inclined to do so,
may all that hear me harden their hearts, and may even
my closest relatives curse my grave!

LEONTES

> The same audacity that allows someone to perform a
> terrible deed also lets her deny it.

HERMIONE

                              That's true enough;
Through 'tis a saying, sir, not due to me.

LEONTES

60   You will not own it.

HERMIONE

                              More than mistress of
Which comes to me in name of fault, I must not
At all acknowledge. For Polixenes,
With whom I am accused, I do confess
65   I loved him as in honour he required,
With such a kind of love as might become
A lady like me, with a love even such,
So and no other, as yourself commanded:
Which not to have done I think had been in me
70   Both disobedience and ingratitude
To you and toward your friend, whose love had spoke,
Even since it could speak, from an infant, freely
That it was yours. Now, for conspiracy,
I know not how it tastes; though it be dish'd
75   For me to try how: all I know of it
Is that Camillo was an honest man;
And why he left your court, the gods themselves,
Wotting no more than I, are ignorant.

LEONTES

You knew of his departure, as you know
80   What you have underta'en to do in 's absence.

HERMIONE

Sir,
You speak a language that I understand not:
My life stands in the level of your dreams,
Which I'll lay down.

LEONTES

85   Your actions are my dreams;
You had a bastard by Polixenes,
And I but dream'd it. As you were past all shame,—

HERMIONE

That's true enough, but that has nothing to do with me.

LEONTES

You won't admit it.

HERMIONE

I take full ownership of my faults, but I won't acknowledge any faults that aren't mine. I confess that I loved Polixenes in the manner his honor required, and with a love that was befitting a lady like me—with such a love, even as you yourself commanded. If I hadn't loved him in this way, I would have been disobeying you and showing ingratitude to both you and your friend, who has loved you since childhood. Now, as for conspiracy, I don't even know what it is like, even if it is being aimed at me. All I know is that Camillo was an honest man, and the gods know as little as I do about why he left your court.

LEONTES

You knew that he was leaving, and you know what you have tried to do in his absence.

HERMIONE

Sir, I don't understand what you are saying. I'll give up my life, which is the target of your delusions.

LEONTES

My "dreams" are made of your actions. You had a bastard child with Polixenes—maybe I just dreamed it! You are past any shame, as women like you are, or any truth. Just

Those of your fact are so—so past all truth:
Which to deny concerns more than avails; for as
90   Thy brat hath been cast out, like to itself,
No father owning it,—which is, indeed,
More criminal in thee than it,—so thou
Shalt feel our justice, in whose easiest passage
Look for no less than death.

HERMIONE

95   Sir, spare your threats:
The bug which you would fright me with I seek.
To me can life be no commodity:
The crown and comfort of my life, your favour,
I do give lost; for I do feel it gone,
100   But know not how it went. My second joy
And first-fruits of my body, from his presence
I am barr'd, like one infectious. My third comfort
Starr'd most unluckily, is from my breast,
The innocent milk in its most innocent mouth,
105   Haled out to murder: myself on every post
Proclaimed a strumpet: with immodest hatred
The child-bed privilege denied, which 'longs
To women of all fashion; lastly, hurried
Here to this place, i' the open air, before
110   I have got strength of limit. Now, my liege,
Tell me what blessings I have here alive,
That I should fear to die? Therefore proceed.
But yet hear this: mistake me not; no life,
I prize it not a straw, but for mine honour,
115   Which I would free, if I shall be condemn'd
Upon surmises, all proofs sleeping else
But what your jealousies awake, I tell you
'Tis rigor and not law. Your honours all,
I do refer me to the oracle:
120   Apollo be my judge!

as I've cast out your brat, whose lack of a father is more
your fault than the child's, I'll devise a punishment for
you, the least of which will be death.

HERMIONE
Sir, save your threats. I'd seek out the terrible punishment
you threaten me with. Life has no value for me now.
Having your favor was my highest goal and my comfort,
and I give it up as lost now, though I don't know how.
My second joy in life, my first son, is kept from me as
though I have a disease. My third comfort, that unlucky
child with the innocent milk still in its innocent mouth,
has been taken from my breast and dragged out to be
murdered. I've been publicly declared a whore, with
outrageous hatred denied the rest after childbirth that
all women of my rank deserve, and hurried here into
the open air before I've regained my strength. Now, my
lord, tell me what I have to live for, and why I should
fear death. Go ahead. But listen to what I say, which I
say not for the sake of my life but for my honor: If I am
condemned on mere guesses and your jealousy without
any proof, it is merely severity and not justice. Your
honors, I commend myself to the oracle, and let Apollo
be my judge!

FIRST LORD

                    This your request
Is altogether just: therefore bring forth,
And in Apollo's name, his oracle.

                           Exeunt certain Officers

HERMIONE

The Emperor of Russia was my father:
125   O that he were alive, and here beholding
His daughter's trial! that he did but see
The flatness of my misery, yet with eyes
Of pity, not revenge!

    Re-enter OFFICERS, *with* CLEOMENES *and* DION

OFFICER

You here shall swear upon this sword of justice,
130   That you, Cleomenes and Dion, have
Been both at Delphos, and from thence have brought
The seal'd-up oracle, by the hand deliver'd
Of great Apollo's priest; and that, since then,
You have not dared to break the holy seal
135   Nor read the secrets in 't.

CLEOMENES, DION

All this we swear.

LEONTES

Break up the seals and read.

OFFICER

    *(reads) Hermione is chaste; Polixenes blameless; Camillo a
    true subject; Leontes a jealous tyrant; his innocent babe
140   truly begotten; and the king shall live without an heir,
    if that which is lost be not found.*

LORDS

Now blessed be the great Apollo!

HERMIONE

                        Praised!

FIRST LORD

Your request is just. Bring forth the oracle of Apollo.

Some officers exit.

HERMIONE

If only my father, the Emperor of Russia, were alive and could be here to see his daughter's trial! If only he could see my misery with eyes of pity, not revenge!

The OFFICERS *re-enter, with* CLEOMENES *and* DION.

OFFICER

You will swear upon this sword of justice that you, Cleomenes and Dion, have both been to Delphos and have brought back with you the sealed oracle, delivered by great Apollo's priest, and that you have not broken the holy seal nor read the secrets in it.

CLEOMENES AND DION

We swear all this.

LEONTES

Break the seal and read.

OFFICER

(*reads*) *Hermione is chaste, Polixenes is innocent, Camillo is a loyal subject, Leontes is a jealous tyrant, and his innocent baby is legitimately born. The king will live without an heir if the baby that was lost is not found.*

LORDS

Blessed be the great Apollo!

HERMIONE

Praise him!

LEONTES
Hast thou read truth?

OFFICER
145   Ay, my lord; even so as it is here set down.

LEONTES
There is no truth at all i' the oracle:
The sessions shall proceed: this is mere falsehood.

Enter SERVANT

SERVANT
My lord the king, the king!

LEONTES
What is the business?

SERVANT
150   O sir, I shall be hated to report it!
The prince your son, with mere conceit and fear
Of the queen's speed, is gone.

LEONTES
How! gone!

SERVANT
Is dead.

LEONTES
155   Apollo's angry; and the heavens themselves
Do strike at my injustice.

HERMIONE *swoons*

How now there!

PAULINA
This news is mortal to the queen: look down
And see what death is doing.

LEONTES
160   Take her hence.
Her heart is but o'ercharged; she will recover.
I have too much believed mine own suspicion.

LEONTES

> Have you read the truth?

OFFICER

> Yes, my lord, exactly as it is written here.

LEONTES

> There is no truth in what the oracle says. The trial will proceed. These are simply lies.

A SERVANT *enters.*

SERVANT

> My lord the king!

LEONTES

> What's going on?

SERVANT

> Sir, you'll hate me when I tell you! The prince, your son, imagining and fearing the queen's fate, is gone.

LEONTES

> What? Gone?

SERVANT

> He's dead.

LEONTES

> Apollo is angry, and the heavens themselves strike back at my injustice.

HERMIONE *swoons.*

> What now?

PAULINA

> The news is deadly to the queen. Look at her and see how she is dying.

LEONTES

> Take her out of here. She's just overwhelmed, she'll get better. I've believed too firmly in my own suspicions. Please, give her something to help her recover.

Beseech you, tenderly apply to her
Some remedies for life.

Exeunt PAULINA *and Ladies, with* HERMIONE

165   Apollo, pardon
My great profaneness 'gainst thine oracle!
I'll reconcile me to Polixenes,
New woo my queen, recall the good Camillo,
Whom I proclaim a man of truth, of mercy;
170   For, being transported by my jealousies
To bloody thoughts and to revenge, I chose
Camillo for the minister to poison
My friend Polixenes: which had been done,
But that the good mind of Camillo tardied
175   My swift command, though I with death and with
Reward did threaten and encourage him,
Not doing 't and being done: he, most humane
And fill'd with honour, to my kingly guest
Unclasp'd my practise, quit his fortunes here,
180   Which you knew great, and to the hazard
Of all encertainties himself commended,
No richer than his honour: how he glisters
Thorough my rust! and how his pity
Does my deeds make the blacker!

Re-enter PAULINA

PAULINA
185   Woe the while!
O, cut my lace, lest my heart, cracking it,
Break too.

FIRST LORD
              What fit is this, good lady?

PAULINA *and the ladies exit with* HERMIONE.

Apollo, forgive how I have insulted your oracle! I'll make it up to Polixenes, court my queen again, and call back good Camillo, whom I declare an honest and merciful man. When I was made mad by my jealousies and plotted bloody revenge, I asked Camillo to poison my friend Polixenes. It would have been done if Camillo hadn't delayed doing it, even though I threatened to kill him if he didn't and to reward him if he did. Even so, he was so humane and honorable that he revealed my plot, left his great fortunes here, and, giving himself over to uncertainty, departed with only his honor. How much finer he appears next to me! And how his good deeds make my actions seem even worse!

PAULINA *re-enters.*

PAULINA

Alas! Cut my corset, so that my heart, in cracking through it, won't break as well.

FIRST LORD

What is wrong, good lady?

PAULINA

What studied torments, tyrant, hast for me?

190   What wheels? racks? fires? what flaying? boiling?

In leads or oils? what old or newer torture

Must I receive, whose every word deserves

To taste of thy most worst? Thy tyranny

Together working with thy jealousies,

195   Fancies too weak for boys, too green and idle

For girls of nine, O, think what they have done

And then run mad indeed, stark mad! for all

Thy by-gone fooleries were but spices of it.

That thou betray'dst Polixenes, 'twas nothing;

200   That did but show thee, of a fool, inconstant

And damnable ingrateful: nor was 't much,

Thou wouldst have poison'd good Camillo's honour,

To have him kill a king: poor trespasses,

More monstrous standing by: whereof I reckon

205   The casting forth to crows thy baby-daughter

To be or none or little; though a devil

Would have shed water out of fire ere done 't:

Nor is 't directly laid to thee, the death

Of the young prince, whose honourable thoughts,

210   Thoughts high for one so tender, cleft the heart

That could conceive a gross and foolish sire

Blemish'd his gracious dam: this is not, no,

Laid to thy answer: but the last,—O lords,

When I have said, cry 'woe!' the queen, the queen,

215   The sweet'st, dear'st creature's dead, and vengeance for 't

Not dropp'd down yet.

FIRST LORD

                    The higher powers forbid!

PAULINA

I say she's dead; I'll swear 't. If word nor oath

Prevail not, go and see: if you can bring

220   Tincture or lustre in her lip, her eye,

Heat outwardly or breath within, I'll serve you

PAULINA

How have you decided to torment me, tyrant? With
wheels, racks, fires, or flaying? With lead or oil?
What old or new torture must I receive, since my
every word deserves the worst you could give me?
Think of what your jealousy—which is too silly
even for boys, and too immature and foolish for
a nine-year-old girl—together with your tyranny
has done, and then you'll go mad! All of your
earlier insanities were just a foretaste of this. Your
betrayal of Polixenes was nothing—it just showed
you to be a fickle and ungrateful fool. Neither was
it much that you tried to tarnish Camillo's honor
by commissioning him to assassinate a king. These
are just small misdeeds, with a more monstrous one
waiting. I suppose the fact that you threw your baby
daughter to the crows is little or nothing beside this,
even though a devil would have shed tears from his
fiery eyes before he did that. And the death of the
young prince isn't directly your fault. His heart tore
in two at the thought that his gracious mother had
been so disgraced by his vulgar and foolish father.
This is not the worst act you'll have to answer for.
But this last deed—oh, lords, when I have told you to
grieve, it is because the queen, that dearest, sweetest
creature, is dead, and she has not yet been avenged.

> All are forms
> of torture.

FIRST LORD

The gods forbid!

PAULINA

I swear that she is dead. If my word and oath don't
convince you, go look. If you can bring any color or life to
her lip or her eye, warm her body or cause her to breathe
again, I'll serve you as I would serve the gods. But, oh,

As I would do the gods. But, O thou tyrant!
Do not repent these things, for they are heavier
Than all thy woes can stir; therefore betake thee
225   To nothing but despair. A thousand knees
Ten thousand years together, naked, fasting,
Upon a barren mountain and still winter
In storm perpetual, could not move the gods
To look that way thou wert.

LEONTES

230   Go on, go on
Thou canst not speak too much; I have deserved
All tongues to talk their bitterest.

FIRST LORD

                             Say no more:
Howe'er the business goes, you have made fault
235   I' the boldness of your speech.

PAULINA

                       I am sorry for 't:
All faults I make, when I shall come to know them,
I do repent. Alas! I have show'd too much
The rashness of a woman: he is touch'd
240   To the noble heart. What's gone and what's past help
Should be past grief: do not receive affliction
At my petition; I beseech you, rather
Let me be punish'd, that have minded you
Of what you should forget. Now, good my liege
245   Sir, royal sir, forgive a foolish woman:
The love I bore your queen—lo, fool again!—
I'll speak of her no more, nor of your children;
I'll not remember you of my own lord,
Who is lost too: take your patience to you,
250   And I'll say nothing.

LEONTES

                    Thou didst speak but well
When most the truth; which I receive much better
Than to be pitied of thee. Prithee, bring me

you tyrant! Don't try to repent now, because all your
sorrow won't change it. All you can do now is despair.
If you had ten thousand years to spend naked, on your
knees, fasting on a barren, wintry mountain in perpetual
storms, the gods wouldn't take pity on you.

LEONTES

Go on, you can't say too much. I've deserved all the
bitterest words people can say.

FIRST LORD

Don't say any more. However it happened, you are
wrong to speak so boldly.

PAULINA

I'm sorry for it. I always repent for my faults once I am
aware of them. Alas! I have been too rash, and he feels it
in his heart. What has happened and can't be fixed should
be past grieving over. Don't let my words make you feel
bad. I beg you, instead, to punish me for reminding you
of what you should forget. Now, my good and royal sir,
forgive a foolish woman. The love I had for your queen—
ah, I'm behaving like a fool again!—I won't speak about
her anymore, or of your children, and I won't remind
you of my husband, who is gone, too. Be patient, and I'll
be quiet.

LEONTES

You spoke best when you told the truth, and I prefer
it to being pitied. Please, take me to the dead bodies of
my queen and son. I'll bury them in one grave, and I'll

To the dead bodies of my queen and son:
255   One grave shall be for both: upon them shall
The causes of their death appear, unto
Our shame perpetual. Once a day I'll visit
The chapel where they lie, and tears shed there
Shall be my recreation: so long as nature
260   Will bear up with this exercise, so long
I daily vow to use it. Come and lead me
Unto these sorrows.

Exeunt

inscribe their gravestone with the cause of their death, to memorialize my shame. I'll visit the chapel where they lie daily, and my pastime will be to shed tears. I'll do it daily, as long as I am able to. Come, take me to this sorrowful sight.

They exit.

ACT 3, SCENE 3

Bohemia. A desert country near the sea.
Enter ANTIGONUS *with a child, and a* MARINER

ANTIGONUS
>Thou art perfect then, our ship hath touch'd upon
>The deserts of Bohemia?

MARINER
>   Ay, my lord: and fear
>We have landed in ill time: the skies look grimly
5 And threaten present blusters. In my conscience,
>The heavens with that we have in hand are angry
>And frown upon 's.

ANTIGONUS
>Their sacred wills be done! Go, get aboard;
>Look to thy bark: I'll not be long before
10 I call upon thee.

MARINER
>   Make your best haste, and go not
>Too far i' the land: 'tis like to be loud weather;
>Besides, this place is famous for the creatures
>Of prey that keep upon 't.

ANTIGONUS
>   Go thou away:
15 I'll follow instantly.

MARINER
>   I am glad at heart
>To be so rid o' the business.

>   *Exit*

ANTIGONUS
>   Come, poor babe:
20 I have heard, but not believed, the spirits o' the dead
>May walk again: if such thing be, thy mother
>Appear'd to me last night, for ne'er was dream

ACT 3, SCENE 3

Bohemia, a desert country near the sea.
ANTIGONUS, *who is carrying a child, and a* MARINER *enter.*

ANTIGONUS

You are sure that our ship has landed at the desert
of Bohemia?

MARINER

Yes, my lord, and I fear we've landed at a bad time. The
sky is dark, and it looks as though a storm approaches.
It seems to me that the heavens are angry at what we are
about to do and are unhappy with us.

ANTIGONUS

Let their sacred will be done! Go aboard, and see to your
ship. I'll call for you shortly.

MARINER

Go as quickly as you can, and don't venture too far
inland. It promises to be a dreadful storm, and this area is
famous for its predators.

ANTIGONUS

Go away. I'll be right behind you.

MARINER

I'm happy to be done with this business.

He exits.

ANTIGONUS

Come, poor child. I've heard but never believed that
the spirits of the dead might walk the Earth. But
perhaps it is true, because last night your mother
appeared to me, and no dream ever seemed so real.

So like a waking. To me comes a creature,
Sometimes her head on one side, some another;
25   I never saw a vessel of like sorrow,
So fill'd and so becoming: in pure white robes,
Like very sanctity, she did approach
My cabin where I lay; thrice bow'd before me,
And gasping to begin some speech, her eyes
30   Became two spouts: the fury spent, anon
Did this break-from her: 'Good Antigonus,
Since fate, against thy better disposition,
Hath made thy person for the thrower-out
Of my poor babe, according to thine oath,
35   Places remote enough are in Bohemia,
There weep and leave it crying; and, for the babe
Is counted lost for ever, Perdita,
I prithee, call 't. For this ungentle business
Put on thee by my lord, thou ne'er shalt see
40   Thy wife Paulina more.' And so, with shrieks
She melted into air. Affrighted much,
I did in time collect myself and thought
This was so and no slumber. Dreams are toys:
Yet for this once, yea, superstitiously,
45   I will be squared by this. I do believe
Hermione hath suffer'd death, and that
Apollo would, this being indeed the issue
Of King Polixenes, it should here be laid,
Either for life or death, upon the earth
50   Of its right father. Blossom, speed thee well!
There lie, and there thy character: there these;
Which may, if fortune please, both breed thee, pretty,
And still rest thine. The storm begins; poor wretch,
That for thy mother's fault art thus exposed
55   To loss and what may follow! Weep I cannot,
But my heart bleeds; and most accursed am I
To be by oath enjoin'd to this. Farewell!
The day frowns more and more: thou 'rt like to have

She comes to me with her head to one side or the other, and I've never seen anyone so filled with sorrow and so beautiful. Dressed in pure white robes, she came to my room where I was resting. She bowed three times to me, and, struggling to speak, she broke into tears. Once her fury was spent, these words came out: "Good Antigonus, since fate, against your good nature, has chosen you to cast out my child according to your oath, leave her in the remote places of Bohemia. There you weep, and leave the child crying. Since she is lost forever, I ask you to call her **Perdita**. Because of this terrible business forced upon you, you will never see your wife Paulina again." And then she disappeared, shrieking. Very frightened, I finally got myself together and decided it had truly happened and wasn't a dream. Dreams are just trifles, but for this once, even if it's superstition, I'll be ruled by one. I believe that Hermione has died, and that this child is truly the child of King Polixenes, so Apollo would want her to be left, whether for life or death, on the land of her real father. Blossom, fare you well! (*he lays down the child and a scroll*) Lie there, and I'll put an account of your parentage with you. (*he puts down a box*) These jewels and gold will help pay for your upbringing, and if fortune pleases, leave some left over for you. (*thunder*) The storm is beginning. Poor child, because of your mother's transgressions you are left out to die! I can't weep, but my heart bleeds, and I'm cursed for having to do this deed. Farewell! The day gets worse and worse. You are likely to be lulled to sleep with a rough lullaby. I've never seen the sky look so dark during the day. What a savage noise! I'll be lucky to get on board! This is the hunt! I'm gone forever.

Latin for "lost one."

He exits, chased by a bear.

A lullaby too rough: I never saw
60   The heavens so dim by day. A savage clamour!
Well may I get aboard! This is the chase:
I am gone for ever.

Exit, pursued by a bear

Enter a SHEPHERD

SHEPHERD
I would there were no age between sixteen and three-
and-twenty, or that youth would sleep out the rest; for
65   there is nothing in the between but getting wenches with
child, wronging the ancientry, stealing, fighting—Hark
you now! Would any but these boiled brains of nineteen
and two-and-twenty hunt this weather? They have scared
away two of my best sheep, which I fear the wolf will
70   sooner find than the master: if any where I have them, 'tis
by the seaside, browsing of ivy. Good luck, an 't be thy
will what have we here! Mercy on 's, a barne a very pretty
barne! A boy or a child, I wonder? A pretty one; a very
pretty one: sure, some 'scape: though I am not bookish,
75   yet I can read waiting-gentlewoman in the 'scape. This
has been some stair-work, some trunk-work, some
behind-door-work: they were warmer that got this than
the poor thing is here. I'll take it up for pity: yet I'll
tarry till my son come; he hallooed but even now. Whoa,
80   ho, hoa!

Enter CLOWN

CLOWN
Hilloa, loa!
SHEPHERD
What, art so near? If thou 'lt see a thing to talk on when
thou art dead and rotten, come hither. What ailest
thou, man?

A **SHEPHERD** *enters.*

SHEPHERD

I wish that the ages between sixteen and twenty-three
didn't exist, or that young men would spend them asleep.
Otherwise there is nothing between those ages but
getting girls pregnant, acting dishonestly toward their
elders, stealing, fighting—look at this! Would anyone
but an addlebrained nineteen- or twenty-two-year-old
hunt in this weather? They've scared away two of my best
sheep, which I'm afraid the wolf will find before I do. If I
find them anywhere it'll be by the shore, eating ivy. What
is this here? Mercy, it's a baby, a pretty baby! A boy or
a girl, I wonder? A pretty one, a very pretty one. Here is
the product of some forbidden affair. I'm not a scholar,
but I can read the signs of a lady-in-waiting behind this.
It must have been some secret sexual relationship carried
out in back stairs, in large chests, or behind closed doors.
The man and woman who conceived this child were more
hot-blooded than the poor baby is. Out of pity I'll take it,
but I'll wait here until my son comes. I heard him shout
just a moment ago. Hallo!

A **YOKEL** *enters.*

YOKEL

Hallo!

> Derogatory
> name for an
> unsophisticated
> person from
> the country.

SHEPHERD

What, are you near? If you want to see something to talk
about when you are dead and rotten, come here. What is
wrong with you?

CLOWN

85   I have seen two such sights, by sea and by land! but I
am not to say it is a sea, for it is now the sky: betwixt the
firmament and it you cannot thrust a bodkin's point.

SHEPHERD

Why, boy, how is it?

CLOWN

I would you did but see how it chafes, how it rages, how
90   it takes up the shore! but that's not the point. O, the most
piteous cry of the poor souls! Sometimes to see 'em, and
not to see 'em; now the ship boring the moon with her
main-mast, and anon swallowed with yest and froth, as
you'd thrust a cork into a hogshead. And then for the
95   land-service, to see how the bear tore out his shoulder-
bone; how he cried to me for help and said his name was
Antigonus, a nobleman. But to make an end of the ship,
to see how the sea flap-dragoned it: but, first, how the
poor souls roared, and the sea mocked them; and how the
100   poor gentleman roared and the bear mocked him, both
roaring louder than the sea or weather.

SHEPHERD

Name of mercy, when was this, boy?

CLOWN

Now, now: I have not winked since I saw these sights: the
men are not yet cold under water, nor the bear half dined
105   on the gentleman: he's at it now.

SHEPHERD

Would I had been by, to have helped the old man!

CLOWN

I would you had been by the ship side, to have helped
her: there your charity would have lacked footing.

SHEPHERD

Heavy matters! heavy matters! but look thee here, boy.
110   Now bless thyself: thou mettest with things dying, I

YOKEL

> I've seen two such sights, on sea and on land! But I won't say it is a sea, since the sky is just as wet from the storm. You couldn't squeeze a needle's point between the sky and the sea.

SHEPHERD

> Why, boy, what's happening there?

YOKEL

> I wish you could see how it rages and rushes up the shore! But that's not the point. Oh, the pitiful cries of the men, coming in and out of sight. Then the ship would rise up so its mast looked like it hit the moon, and the next moment it was swallowed by the frothing waves. And then on land, I saw how the bear tore out his shoulder, and he cried to me for help. He said his name was Antigonus, and he was a nobleman. But to finish telling you about the ship, you should have seen how the sea swallowed it up. But first the poor men roared, and the sea mocked them, and then the poor gentleman roared, and the bear mocked him, and they both roared louder than either the sea or the storm.

SHEPHERD

> Goodness me, when did this happen?

YOKEL

> Just now—I haven't even blinked since I saw these sights. The men aren't yet cold under the water, and the bear has only partly dined on the gentleman—he's still eating now.

SHEPHERD

> If only I'd been close by to help the gentleman!

YOKEL

> I wish you had been near the ship so you could have helped it—on the water you wouldn't have had a place to stand.

SHEPHERD

> Sad affairs, sad affairs! But look here, boy. Say a blessing. While you were watching things dying, I

with things newborn. Here's a sight for thee; look thee, a
bearing-cloth for a squire's child! look thee here; take up,
take up, boy; open 't. So, let's see: it was told me I should
be rich by the fairies. This is some changeling: open 't.
115   What's within, boy?

CLOWN

You're a made old man: if the sins of your youth are
forgiven you, you're well to live. Gold! all gold!

SHEPHERD

This is fairy gold, boy, and 'twill prove so: up with 't,
keep it close: home, home, the next way. We are lucky,
120   boy; and to be so still requires nothing but secrecy. Let
my sheep go: come, good boy, the next way home.

CLOWN

Go you the next way with your findings. I'll go see if the
bear be gone from the gentleman and how much he hath
eaten: they are never curst but when they are hungry: if
125   there be any of him left, I'll bury it.

SHEPHERD

That's a good deed. If thou mayest discern by that which
is left of him what he is, fetch me to the sight of him.

CLOWN

Marry, will I; and you shall help to put him i' the ground.

SHEPHERD

'Tis a lucky day, boy, and we'll do good deeds on 't.

Exeunt

was meeting with things newly born. Here's a sight for you. Look, baby clothes for a **squire's child!** Look here, pick it up, boy, and open it. Let's see what's in it. I've been told that the fairies would make me rich. This is some **changeling**. Open it. What's in it, boy?

A squire was a man of relatively high social standing.

A child said to have been swapped for another child by fairies.

YOKEL

You are set, old man! As long as the sins of your youth have been forgiven, you'll live well. It's gold, all gold!

SHEPHERD

This is fairy gold, boy, and will prove to be. Pick it up, and hold it close. Let's go home. We are lucky, boy, and to keep it that way we have to keep this matter a secret. Let the sheep go. Come, good boy, let's go home.

YOKEL

Go home yourself with what you've found. I'll go see if the bear has left the gentleman and how much of him he ate. They are only vicious when they are hungry. If there is anything left of the gentleman, I'll bury it.

SHEPHERD

That's a good deed. If you can tell by what's left of him who he was, bring me to the body.

YOKEL

I will, and then you can help me bury him.

SHEPHERD

It's a lucky day, boy, and we'll do good deeds to mark it.

They exit.

ACT FOUR
SCENE 1

Enter TIME, *the Chorus*

TIME

I, that please some, try all, both joy and terror
Of good and bad, that makes and unfolds error,
Now take upon me, in the name of Time,
To use my wings. Impute it not a crime
5   To me or my swift passage, that I slide
O'er sixteen years and leave the growth untried
Of that wide gap, since it is in my power
To o'erthrow law and in one self-born hour
To plant and o'erwhelm custom. Let me pass
10   The same I am, ere ancient'st order was
Or what is now received: I witness to
The times that brought them in; so shall I do
To the freshest things now reigning and make stale
The glistering of this present, as my tale
15   Now seems to it. Your patience this allowing,
I turn my glass and give my scene such growing
As you had slept between: Leontes leaving,
The effects of his fond jealousies so grieving
That he shuts up himself, imagine me,
20   Gentle spectators, that I now may be
In fair Bohemia, and remember well,
I mentioned a son o' the king's, which Florizel
I now name to you; and with speed so pace
To speak of Perdita, now grown in grace
25   Equal with wondering: what of her ensues
I list not prophecy; but let Time's news
Be known when 'tis brought forth.
A shepherd's daughter,
And what to her adheres, which follows after,

ACT FOUR
SCENE 1

TIME *enters as the chorus.*

TIME

I am taking up my wings, in the name of Time,
which pleases some, tests all, brings both joy and
terror, makes errors and corrects them. Don't see
it as a crime that I pass quickly over sixteen years
and leave that wide gap unexamined, as I have
the power to overthrow the laws of nature and, in
one hour, to establish or topple custom. Let me
remain as I've been since before civilization began
through what currently is. I saw the times that led
to the present, and, as I did to the past, I'll make
the youngest things old and dim the shine of the
present until it, too, is old. If your patience allows,
I'll turn my hourglass and move the scene forward
as if you had slept through it all. Leontes mourns
the terrible results of his foolish jealousy so much
that he shuts himself away. Then imagine, dear
spectators, that I am now in fair Bohemia, where a
son of the king, named Florizel, lives. And quickly
I'll speak of Perdita, grown into a young woman so
graceful she inspires admiration. I won't prophesy
what will happen to her, but let Time reveal it. She is
a shepherd's daughter, and what pertains to her is the
provenance of Time.

Time was frequently depicted as an old bald man with wings, sometimes carrying an hourglass and a scythe. In ancient Greek tragedy, the chorus was a group of performers who were part of the play and commented on the main action.

30   Is the argument of Time. Of this allow,
        If ever you have spent time worse ere now;
        If never, yet that Time himself doth say
        He wishes earnestly you never may.

                                                        Exit

Allow this leap in time if ever before now you've
spent time in a worse way. If you haven't, Time
himself hopes you never will.

He exits.

ACT 4, SCENE 2

Bohemia. The palace of POLIXENES.
Enter POLIXENES *and* CAMILLO

POLIXENES

I pray thee, good Camillo, be no more importunate: 'tis a
sickness denying thee any thing; a death to grant this.

CAMILLO

It is sixteen years since I saw my country: though I have
for the most part been aired abroad, I desire to lay my
bones there. Besides, the penitent king, my master, hath
sent for me; to whose feeling sorrows I might be some
allay, or I o'erween to think so, which is another spur to
my departure.

POLIXENES

As thou lovest me, Camillo, wipe not out the rest of thy
services by leaving me now: the need I have of thee thine
own goodness hath made; better not to have had thee
than thus to want thee: thou, having made me businesses
which none without thee can sufficiently manage, must
either stay to execute them thyself or take away with
thee the very services thou hast done; which if I have not
enough considered, as too much I cannot, to be more
thankful to thee shall be my study, and my profit therein
the heaping friendships. Of that fatal country, Sicilia,
prithee speak no more; whose very naming punishes me
with the remembrance of that penitent, as thou callest
him, and reconciled king, my brother; whose loss of his
most precious queen and children are even now to be
afresh lamented. Say to me, when sawest thou the Prince
Florizel, my son? Kings are no less unhappy, their issue
not being gracious, than they are in losing them when
they have approved their virtues.

ACT 4, SCENE 2

Bohemia. The palace of POLIXENES.
POLIXENES *and* CAMILLO *enter.*

POLIXENES

I beg you, Camillo, stop being so persistent. It's terrible
to deny you anything, but it would be death to grant this.

CAMILLO

It's been sixteen years since I've seen my country.
Although I've lived abroad so long, I want to be buried
at home. Besides, my master, the king, regrets his actions
and has sent for me. Perhaps I can ease his grief, if I'm
not too presumptuous in thinking I might, and that
makes my departure all the more urgent.

POLIXENES

If you love me, Camillo, don't renounce the rest of your
service to me by leaving me now. It's your own excellence
that makes me need you so much. It would have been
better not to have known you at all than to miss you.
Since you've managed matters here in a way that no one
can do without you, you must either stay and see them
through or take them with you. If I haven't been thankful
enough—and I can't be too thankful—I'll apply myself to
it even more and find my profit in your great friendship.
Please don't speak of that deadly country, Sicilia,
anymore. Its very name hurts by making me remember
that remorseful—as you call him—and reconciled king,
whose loss of his precious queen and children should be
mourned anew even now. Tell me, when did you last see
my son, Prince Florizel? Kings are just as unhappy when
their children are not virtuous as when they lose them
after they've proved their virtues.

CAMILLO

Sir, it is three days since I saw the prince. What his
happier affairs may be, are to me unknown: but I have
missingly noted, he is of late much retired from court and
30   is less frequent to his princely exercises than formerly he
hath appeared.

POLIXENES

I have considered so much, Camillo, and with some care;
so far that I have eyes under my service which look upon
his removedness; from whom I have this intelligence, that
35   he is seldom from the house of a most homely shepherd;
a man, they say, that from very nothing, and beyond
the imagination of his neighbours, is grown into an
unspeakable estate.

CAMILLO

I have heard, sir, of such a man, who hath a daughter of
40   most rare note: the report of her is extended more than
can be thought to begin from such a cottage.

POLIXENES

That's likewise part of my intelligence; but, I fear, the
angle that plucks our son thither. Thou shalt accompany
us to the place; where we will, not appearing what we
45   are, have some question with the shepherd; from whose
simplicity I think it not uneasy to get the cause of my
son's resort thither. Prithee, be my present partner in this
business, and lay aside the thoughts of Sicilia.

CAMILLO

I willingly obey your command.

POLIXENES

50   My best Camillo! We must disguise ourselves.

Exeunt

CAMILLO

Sir, it has been three days since I saw the prince. I don't know what happiness he might have, but I have noticed that lately he's more often absent from the court and neglectful of his princely duties than in the past.

POLIXENES

I have thought about this, and with some concern, Camillo, so much so that I've had some of my servants keep an eye on him while he's been absent. From them I've learned that he is often at the home of a simple shepherd, a man, they say, who has gone from nothing to amazing riches, greater than any of his neighbors could have imagined.

CAMILLO

I've heard of such a man, sir, who has a most exceptional daughter. What people say of her is beyond what one would expect to have come from such a cottage.

POLIXENES

I've heard the same thing, and I fear that she's what takes my son there. You shall go with me to that place, and in disguise we'll question the shepherd, whose simple nature I think will make it easy to find out why my son visits there. Please, be my partner in this matter and forget about Sicilia.

CAMILLO

I willingly obey your command.

POLIXENES

Wonderful Camillo! We must disguise ourselves.

They exit.

ACT 4, SCENE 3

A road near the SHEPHERD*'s cottage.*
Enter AUTOLYCUS*, singing*

AUTOLYCUS

>When daffodils begin to peer,
>>With heigh! the doxy over the dale,
>Why, then comes in the sweet o' the year;
>>For the red blood reigns in the winter's pale.

5

>The white sheet bleaching on the hedge,
>>With heigh! the sweet birds, O, how they sing!
>Doth set my pugging tooth on edge;
>>For a quart of ale is a dish for a king.

10

>The lark, that tirra-lyra chants,
>>With heigh! with heigh! the thrush and the jay,
>Are summer songs for me and my aunts,
>>While we lie tumbling in the hay.

15

I have served Prince Florizel and in my time wore three-
pile; but now I am out of service:

>But shall I go mourn for that, my dear?
>>The pale moon shines by night:
>And when I wander here and there,
>>I then do most go right.

20

>If tinkers may have leave to live,
>>And bear the sow-skin budget,
>Then my account I well may, give,
>>And in the stocks avouch it.

25

My traffic is sheets; when the kite builds, look to lesser
linen. My father named me Autolycus; who being, as I

30

ACT 4, SCENE 3

A road near the SHEPHERD'S *cottage.*
AUTOLYCUS *enters, singing.*

AUTOLYCUS

> *When daffodils begin to sprout,*
> > *With the poor wench over the hills,*
> *Why then it's the sweetest part of the year as red blood*
> > *Reigns in flesh made pale by winter.*

> *The white sheet airing out on the hedge,*
> > *And oh, the sweet birds singing,*
> *Makes my thieving fingers itch,*
> > *And a quart of beer is a drink for a king!*

> *The lark chants "tirra-lyra,"*
> > *And the thrush and the jay sing,*
> *While my mistress and I*
> > *Tumble about in the hay.*

I have served Prince Florizel and worn **three-piled velvet**, but now I'm unemployed.

A luxuriously thick type of velvet.

> *But should I mourn for that, my dear?*
> > *The pale moon shines at night,*
> *And in wandering here and there,*
> > *I take the right course through life.*

> *If menders of metal pots have the right to live*
> > *And bear the burden of their tool bag,*
> *Then I can tell my own story*
> > *And in **the stocks**.*

A form of punishment in which a person was locked into a wooden device, called the stocks, in public to be exposed to ridicule.

I deal in sheets, and when the thieving bird builds his nest, he takes up poorer linen. My father named me

am, littered under Mercury, was likewise a snapper-up
of unconsidered trifles. With die and drab I purchased
this caparison, and my revenue is the silly cheat. Gallows
and knock are too powerful on the highway: beating and
35   hanging are terrors to me: for the life to come, I sleep out
the thought of it. A prize! a prize!

Enter CLOWN

CLOWN

Let me see: every 'leven wether tods; every tod yields
pound and odd shilling; fifteen hundred shorn. What
comes the wool to?

AUTOLYCUS

40   (*aside*) If the springe hold, the cock's mine.

CLOWN

I cannot do 't without counters. Let me see; what am I to
buy for our sheep-shearing feast? Three pound of sugar,
five pound of currants, rice,—what will this sister of mine
do with rice? But my father hath made her mistress of
45   the feast, and she lays it on. She hath made me four and
twenty nose-gays for the shearers, three-man-song-men
all, and very good ones; but they are most of them means
and bases; but one puritan amongst them, and he sings
psalms to horn-pipes. I must have saffron to colour the
50   warden pies; mace; dates?—none, that's out of my note;
nutmegs, seven; a race or two of ginger, but that I may
beg; four pound of prunes, and as many of raisins o'
the sun.

AUTOLYCUS

(*grovelling on the ground*) O that ever I was born!

CLOWN

55   I' the name of me—

Autolycus. Like me he was born under **Mercury**, and like me he would steal those little things left unsecured By gambling and pimping I bought this outfit, and my income is from little deceptions. Being a highwayman might get me hanged or beat, which are terrors to me, and as for the afterlife, I try not to think about it. Oh, look—a prize!

In Greek myth, Autolycus was the grandfather of Odysseus and a cunning thief. Mercury was the Roman god of thieves.

The YOKEL *enters.*

YOKEL

Let's see. Every eleven sheep gives about twenty-eight pounds of wool. Every twenty-eight pounds of wool earns a pound and some shillings. If we've shorn fifteen hundred sheep, how much does that come to?

AUTOLYCUS

(*aside*) If the trap holds, the bird is mine.

YOKEL

I can't do it without something to add it up. Let's see, what do I need to buy for our **sheep-shearing feast**? Three pounds of sugar, five pounds of currants, rice. What does my sister need rice for? But my father has put her in charge of the feast, and she is doing a good job with it. She's made twenty-four small bouquets for the shearers, who can all sing three-part songs, and very well. But they are mostly tenors and basses, and one is so saintly he sings psalms for dances. I have to get saffron to color the pear pies. Do I need **mace** and dates? No, that's not on my list. Seven nutmegs, some ginger root—though I might be able to get that for free—and four pounds each of prunes and raisins.

A traditional summer event in rural England at the time.

A spice derived from the same fruit as nutmeg.

AUTOLYCUS

Oh, that I was ever born! (*he lies flat on the ground*)

YOKEL

What in the world—

AUTOLYCUS

O, help me, help me! pluck but off these rags; and then,
death, death!

CLOWN

Alack, poor soul! thou hast need of more rags to lay on
thee, rather than have these off.

AUTOLYCUS

60 O sir, the loathsomeness of them offends me more
than the stripes I have received, which are mighty ones
and millions.

CLOWN

Alas, poor man! a million of beating may come to a
great matter.

AUTOLYCUS

65 I am robbed, sir, and beaten; my money and apparel ta'en
from me, and these detestable things put upon me.

CLOWN

What, by a horseman, or a footman?

AUTOLYCUS

A footman, sweet sir, a footman.

CLOWN

Indeed, he should be a footman by the garments he has
70 left with thee: if this be a horseman's coat, it hath seen
very hot service. Lend me thy hand, I'll help thee: come,
lend me thy hand.

AUTOLYCUS

O, good sir, tenderly, O!

CLOWN

Alas, poor soul!

AUTOLYCUS

75 O, good sir, softly, good sir! I fear, sir, my shoulder-blade
is out.

CLOWN

How now! canst stand?

AUTOLYCUS

Oh, help me! Take off these rags, and then I can die!

YOKEL

Alas, poor soul! You need more rags to cover you, not to take your rags off.

AUTOLYCUS

Oh, sir, their awfulness offends me more than the blows I received, which were numerous and painful.

YOKEL

Alas, poor man! To have suffered a million blows is a serious problem.

AUTOLYCUS

I've been robbed, sir, and beaten, my money and clothes taken from me, and these horrible rags put on me instead.

YOKEL

What, by a man on horse, or on foot?

AUTOLYCUS

A man on foot, sweet sir, on foot.

YOKEL

Indeed, he should be a man on foot, judging by those clothes. If it were the coat of a man on a horse, it has seen some terrible service. Give me your hand, and I'll help you. Here, give me your hand.

AUTOLYCUS

Oh, good sir, be gentle!

YOKEL

Alas, poor soul!

AUTOLYCUS

Oh, good sir, carefully! I'm afraid my shoulder might be dislocated.

YOKEL

What else? Can you stand?

AUTOLYCUS

(*picking his pocket*) Softly, dear sir; good sir, softly. You ha' done me a charitable office.

CLOWN

80   Dost lack any money? I have a little money for thee.

AUTOLYCUS

No, good sweet sir; no, I beseech you, sir: I have a kinsman not past three quarters of a mile hence, unto whom I was going; I shall there have money, or any thing I want: offer me no money, I pray you; that kills my heart.

CLOWN

85   What manner of fellow was he that robbed you?

AUTOLYCUS

A fellow, sir, that I have known to go about with troll-my-dames; I knew him once a servant of the prince: I cannot tell, good sir, for which of his virtues it was, but he was certainly whipped out of the court.

CLOWN

90   His vices, you would say; there's no virtue whipped out of the court: they cherish it to make it stay there; and yet it will no more but abide.

AUTOLYCUS

Vices, I would say, sir. I know this man well: he hath been since an ape-bearer; then a process-server, a bailiff; then

95   he compassed a motion of the Prodigal Son, and married a tinker's wife within a mile where my land and living lies; and, having flown over many knavish professions, he settled only in rogue: some call him Autolycus.

CLOWN

Out upon him! prig, for my life, prig: he haunts wakes,

100   fairs and bear-baitings.

AUTOLYCUS

Very true, sir; he, sir, he; that's the rogue that put me into this apparel.

AUTOLYCUS

> (*picking the Yokel's pocket*) Careful, dear sir, careful. You have done me a charitable deed.

YOKEL

> Do you need money? I have a little I can give you.

AUTOLYCUS

> No, good, kind sir, I beg you. I have a relative less than a mile from here whom I was going to visit. He can give me money or whatever I need. Please, don't offer me money. That kills me.

YOKEL

> What did the fellow who robbed you look like?

AUTOLYCUS

> A fellow, sir, that I have known to go about with prostitutes. I know he was once a servant of the prince. I'm not sure, good sir, for which of his virtues it was, but he certainly got whipped out of court.

YOKEL

> Vices, you mean, since virtues aren't whipped out of court. They cherish virtues there, and yet they won't stay there long.

AUTOLYCUS

> I would say vices, sir. I know this man well. Since he left he has been a performer with a monkey, then a summons server, a bailiff, and then he came up with a puppet show about the Prodigal Son, and then he married a pot-mender's wife within a mile of my property. Having entered and abandoned all these disreputable professions, he finally settled on being a rogue. Some call him Autolycus.

YOKEL

> A curse on him! A crook, upon my life, a crook. He lingers about funerals, fairs, and bear-baitings.

AUTOLYCUS

> Very true, sir, that's him, the rogue that put me in these clothes.

CLOWN

Not a more cowardly rogue in all Bohemia: if you had but
looked big and spit at him, he'd have run.

AUTOLYCUS

105   I must confess to you, sir, I am no fighter: I am false of
heart that way; and that he knew, I warrant him.

CLOWN

How do you now?

AUTOLYCUS

Sweet sir, much better than I was; I can stand and walk:
I will even take my leave of you, and pace softly towards
110   my kinsman's.

CLOWN

Shall I bring thee on the way?

AUTOLYCUS

No, good-faced sir; no, sweet sir.

CLOWN

Then fare thee well: I must go buy spices for our sheep-
shearing.

AUTOLYCUS

115   Prosper you, sweet sir!

Exit CLOWN

Your purse is not hot enough to purchase your spice. I'll
be with you at your sheep-shearing too: if I make not this
cheat bring out another and the shearers prove sheep, let
me be unrolled and my name put in the book of virtue!
(Sings)
120   *Jog on, jog on, the foot-path way,*
And merrily hent the stile-a:
A merry heart goes all the day,
Your sad tires in a mile-a.

Exit

YOKEL

> There's no more cowardly rogue in all of Bohemia. If you had looked large and had spit at him, he would have run.

AUTOLYCUS

> I have to confess to you, sir, I'm not a fighter. I'm too faint at heart, and I'm sure he knew it.

YOKEL

> How are you now?

AUTOLYCUS

> Kind sir, much better now than before. I can stand on my own and walk. I'll even say goodbye to you, and make my way carefully to my relative's home.

YOKEL

> Shall I help you there?

AUTOLYCUS

> No, pretty sir. No, kind sir.

YOKEL

> Then best of luck to you. I have to go buy spices for our sheep-shearing.

AUTOLYCUS

> May you prosper, sweet sir!

The YOKEL *exits.*

> Your purse is not full enough to purchase your spices. I'll join you at your sheep-shearing, too. If I don't make this deception lead to another and prove the shearers as stupid as sheep, let me be removed from the list of thieves and my name become known for virtue!
> *(He sings.)*
> *Jog on, jog on, along the footpath,*
> *   And merrily grasp the gate.*
> *A merry heart can go all day,*
> *   A sad heart tires after just a mile.*

He exits.

ACT 4, SCENE 4

The SHEPHERD'*s cottage.*
Enter FLORIZEL *and* PERDITA

FLORIZEL

These your unusual weeds to each part of you
Do give a life: no shepherdess, but Flora
Peering in April's front. This your sheep-shearing
Is as a meeting of the petty gods,
5   And you the queen on 't.

PERDITA

               Sir, my gracious lord,
To chide at your extremes it not becomes me:
O, pardon, that I name them! Your high self,
The gracious mark o' the land, you have obscured
10   With a swain's wearing, and me, poor lowly maid,
Most goddess-like prank'd up: but that our feasts
In every mess have folly and the feeders
Digest it with a custom, I should blush
To see you so attired, swoon, I think,
15   To show myself a glass.

FLORIZEL

                  I bless the time
When my good falcon made her flight across
Thy father's ground.

PERDITA

             Now Jove afford you cause!
20   To me the difference forges dread; your greatness
Hath not been used to fear. Even now I tremble
To think your father, by some accident,
Should pass this way as you did: O, the Fates!
How would he look, to see his work so noble
25   Vilely bound up? What would he say? Or how
Should I, in these my borrow'd flaunts, behold
The sternness of his presence?

ACT 4, SCENE 4

The SHEPHERD's *cottage.*
FLORIZEL *and* PERDITA *enter.*

FLORIZEL

> Your festival clothes give you a new look. No longer a
> shepherdess, but the goddess of flowers appearing at the
> beginning of April. Your sheep-shearing is like a meeting
> of minor gods, and you are the queen of them.

PERDITA

> My gracious lord, it doesn't suit me to rebuke you for
> exaggerations. Oh, pardon me for naming them! You, the
> one whose charms make him admired by the public, have
> hidden yourself in rustic clothing, while I, just a poor,
> lowly girl, am made up like a goddess. If there weren't
> foolishness at every table during our feasts, and if people
> weren't accustomed to such foolishness by now, I'd feel
> embarrassed to see you dressed like that and would faint
> to see myself in the mirror.

FLORIZEL

> I bless the day when my hunting bird flew across your
> father's land.

PERDITA

> Now may Jove give you reason to be glad! For me the
> difference in rank between us fills me with dread, though
> you in your greatness aren't used to fear. Even now I
> tremble to think that your father might by some accident
> pass this way, like you did. Oh, the Fates! How would
> he look when he discovered that his noble son was so
> humbly dressed! What would he say? How should I, in
> this borrowed finery, look upon his stern presence?

FLORIZEL

                              Apprehend
Nothing but jollity. The gods themselves,
30   Humbling their deities to love, have taken
The shapes of beasts upon them: Jupiter
Became a bull, and bellow'd; the green Neptune
A ram, and bleated; and the fire-robed god,
Golden Apollo, a poor humble swain,
35   As I seem now. Their transformations
Were never for a piece of beauty rarer,
Nor in a way so chaste, since my desires
Run not before mine honour, nor my lusts
Burn hotter than my faith.

PERDITA

40   O, but, sir,
Your resolution cannot hold, when 'tis
Opposed, as it must be, by the power of the king:
One of these two must be necessities,
Which then will speak, that you must
45   change this purpose,
Or I my life.

FLORIZEL

                    Thou dearest Perdita,
With these forced thoughts, I prithee, darken not
The mirth o' the feast. Or I'll be thine, my fair,
50   Or not my father's. For I cannot be
Mine own, nor any thing to any, if
I be not thine. To this I am most constant,
Though destiny say no. Be merry, gentle;
Strangle such thoughts as these with any thing
55   That you behold the while. Your guests are coming:
Lift up your countenance, as it were the day
Of celebration of that nuptial which
We two have sworn shall come.

PERDITA

                              O lady Fortune,
60   Stand you auspicious!

FLORIZEL

Imagine only happiness. The gods themselves have taken on the form of beasts when they're in love. Jupiter became a bull and bellowed; Neptune became a ram and bleated. And the god of the sun, golden Apollo, became a humble shepherd just as I appear today. But their transformations were never for someone so beautiful, and neither were their loves as chaste as mine, because my desires are secondary to my honor, and my faith burns hotter than my lusts.

PERDITA

But, sir, your feelings toward me might falter when they are opposed, as they must be, by the power of the king. Then one of the two must happen: either you will change your feelings or I will lose my life.

FLORIZEL

Dearest Perdita, don't let these farfetched thoughts dampen the high spirits of the feast. I'll be yours, my fair love, and not my father's. I can't be myself, or anything to anyone, if I'm not yours. My feelings won't change, even if destiny says we are not to be together. Be happy, dearest. Get rid of these thoughts by busying yourself with something else. Your guests are coming. Look happy, as if it were the day we're getting married, as we've sworn we will.

PERDITA

Oh, Fortune, remain favorable!

FLORIZEL
See, your guests approach:
Address yourself to entertain them sprightly,
And let's be red with mirth.

Enter SHEPHERD, CLOWN, MOPSA, DORCAS, *and others, with*
POLIXENES *and* CAMILLO *disguised*

SHEPHERD
Fie, daughter! when my old wife lived, upon
65   This day she was both pantler, butler, cook,
Both dame and servant; welcomed all, served all;
Would sing her song and dance her turn; now here,
At upper end o' the table, now i' the middle;
On his shoulder, and his; her face o' fire
70   With labour and the thing she took to quench it,
She would to each one sip. You are retired,
As if you were a feasted one and not
The hostess of the meeting: pray you, bid
These unknown friends to 's welcome; for it is
75   A way to make us better friends, more known.
Come, quench your blushes and present yourself
That which you are, mistress o' the feast: come on,
And bid us welcome to your sheep-shearing,
As your good flock shall prosper.

PERDITA
80   *(to Polixenes)*   Sir, welcome:
It is my father's will I should take on me
The hostess-ship o' the day. *(to Camillo)* You're
        welcome, sir.
Give me those flowers there, Dorcas. Reverend sirs,
For you there's rosemary and rue; these keep
85   Seeming and savour all the winter long:
Grace and remembrance be to you both,
And welcome to our shearing!

FLORIZEL

See, your guests are approaching. Prepare yourself to entertain them in a lively manner, and let's be red-faced from all our laughter.

The SHEPHERD, YOKEL, MOPSA, DORCAS, *and others enter.* POLIXENES *and* CAMILLO, *who are in disguise, also enter.*

SHEPHERD

Oh, daughter, when my old wife was still alive, on this day she was a pantry maid, butler, cook, mistress of the house, and servant. She welcomed all, served all, would sing her song and dance her share. She would sit first at the head of the table, then in the middle. She'd be on this man's shoulder, and then on that one's. Her face would be red from work and what she drank to quench her thirst, and she would drink a toast to each person. You are withdrawn, as if you were a guest and not the hostess of this party. Please, welcome these strangers so that we can become better acquainted. Come, stop blushing and present yourself as that which you are: the mistress of the feast. Come on and welcome us to your sheep-shearing, so that your flock will prosper.

PERDITA

(*to Polixenes*) Sir, welcome. My father wishes me to be the hostess here today. (*to Camillo*) You are welcome here, sir. Give me those flowers there, Dorcas. Honored sirs, for you there are **rosemary and rue**, which keep their appearance and scent all through the winter. May you both have grace and remembrance, and welcome to our shearing!

Rosemary is an herb that symbolizes remembrance, while rue is an herb that symbolizes repentance and grace.

POLIXENES

Shepherdess,
A fair one are you—well you fit our ages
90 With flowers of winter.

PERDITA

Sir, the year growing ancient,
Not yet on summer's death, nor on the birth
Of trembling winter, the fairest
flowers o' the season
95 Are our carnations and streak'd gillyvors,
Which some call nature's bastards: of that kind
Our rustic garden's barren; and I care not
To get slips of them.

POLIXENES

Wherefore, gentle maiden,
100 Do you neglect them?

PERDITA

For I have heard it said
There is an art which in their piedness shares
With great creating nature.

POLIXENES

Say there be;
105 Yet nature is made better by no mean
But nature makes that mean: so, over that art
Which you say adds to nature, is an art
That nature makes. You see, sweet maid, we marry
A gentler scion to the wildest stock,
110 And make conceive a bark of baser kind
By bud of nobler race: this is an art
Which does mend nature, change it rather, but
The art itself is nature.

PERDITA

So it is.

POLIXENES

115 Then make your garden rich in gillyvors,
And do not call them bastards.

POLIXENES

Fair shepherdess, since we are old, you do well to pair us with **winter flowers**.

Refers to the common metaphor comparing the stages of life to the seasons, with winter being old age.

PERDITA

Sir, the year is growing old, with the summer not yet over and the winter not yet starting. The fairest flowers of this season are carnations and two-toned gillyflowers, which some call nature's bastards. But we don't have any of those flowers in our garden, and I don't care to get any cuttings of them.

POLIXENES

Kind maiden, why do you reject them?

PERDITA

Because I've heard that their many colors are due as much to cross-breeding as to nature.

POLIXENES

Perhaps that's true. But any technique used to improve nature is itself made by nature, so any form of artifice that adds to nature is really a natural artifice. You see, sweet maid, we marry a more noble stem to a wild stem, so that a lesser plant produces one that is superior. This is an art that improves nature, or rather changes it, but the art itself is natural.

PERDITA

So it is.

POLIXENES

Then fill your garden with gillyflowers, and don't call them bastards.

PERDITA
I'll not put

The dibble in earth to set one slip of them;
No more than were I painted I would wish

120 This youth should say 'twere well and only therefore
Desire to breed by me. Here's flowers for you;
Hot lavender, mints, savoury, marjoram;
The marigold, that goes to bed wi' the sun
And with him rises weeping: these are flowers

125 Of middle summer, and I think they are given
To men of middle age. You're very welcome.

CAMILLO

I should leave grazing, were I of your flock,
And only live by gazing.

PERDITA
Out, alas!

130 You'd be so lean, that blasts of January
Would blow you through and through.
Now, my fair'st friend,
I would I had some flowers o' the spring that might
Become your time of day; and yours, and yours,

135 That wear upon your virgin branches yet
Your maidenheads growing: O Proserpina,
For the flowers now, that frighted thou let'st fall
From Dis's waggon! daffodils,
That come before the swallow dares, and take

140 The winds of March with beauty; violets dim,
But sweeter than the lids of Juno's eyes
Or Cytherea's breath; pale primroses
That die unmarried, ere they can behold
Bight Phoebus in his strength—a malady

145 Most incident to maids; bold oxlips and
The crown imperial; lilies of all kinds,
The flower-de-luce being one! O, these I lack,
To make you garlands of, and my sweet friend,
To strew him o'er and o'er!

PERDITA

> I won't put a shovel in the dirt to plant a single one of
> them, just as I wouldn't want this youth here to think
> I'm attractive and want to sleep with me only because
> I'm wearing makeup. Here are flowers for you: lavender,
> mint, savory, marjoram, and the marigold, which sets
> with the sun and rises with it filled with dew. These are
> flowers that bloom in the middle of summer, and I think
> they should be given to men of middle age. You're very
> welcome here. (*she gives them flowers*)

CAMILLO

> If I were part of your flock, I would stop grazing and
> instead gaze on you as my only nourishment.

PERDITA

> Oh, not at all! You'd be so skinny that the icy
> winds of January would blow right through you.
> (*to Florizel*) Now, my fairest friend, I wish I had
> flowers of the spring that would match your age, (*to
> Mopsa and Dorcas*) and yours, and yours, who are
> still in your adolescence. Oh, **Proserpina, if only
> we had the flowers that you, frightened, let fall
> from Dis's chariot!** Daffodils that bloom before the
> swallows dare return from the south, and that charm
> the winds of March with their beauty. Modest violets
> that are sweeter than **Juno's eyes** or **Cytherea's
> breath**. Pale primroses that die unmarried, before
> they can see the bright sun at full strength—a
> sickness that often affects young women. Bold oxlips
> and the crown imperial lily, lilies of all kinds, the
> **flower-de-luce** being one! Oh, if only I had these
> flowers to make garlands and to throw over my
> sweet friend!

In Greek myth, Proserpina was abducted by Dis, also known as Pluto, while she was collecting flowers.

Juno was the Roman name for Hera, Zeus's wife and queen of the gods. Cytherea is another name for Venus, goddess of love.

Or fleur-de-lis.

FLORIZEL

150   What, like a corse?

PERDITA

No, like a bank for love to lie and play on;
Not like a corse; or if, not to be buried,
But quick and in mine arms. Come, take your flowers:
Methinks I play as I have seen them do
155   In Whitsun pastorals: sure this robe of mine
Does change my disposition.

FLORIZEL

                                    What you do
Still betters what is done. When you speak, sweet.
I'd have you do it ever: when you sing,
160   I'd have you buy and sell so, so give alms,
Pray so; and, for the ordering your affairs,
To sing them too: when you do dance, I wish you
A wave o' the sea, that you might ever do
Nothing but that; move still, still so,
165   And own no other function: each your doing,
So singular in each particular,
Crowns what you are doing in the present deed,
That all your acts are queens.

PERDITA

                                    O Doricles,
170   Your praises are too large: but that your youth,
And the true blood which peepeth fairly through 't,
Do plainly give you out an unstain'd shepherd,
With wisdom I might fear, my Doricles,
You woo'd me the false way.

FLORIZEL

                                    I think you have
175   As little skill to fear as I have purpose
To put you to 't. But come; our dance, I pray:
Your hand, my Perdita: so turtles pair,
That never mean to part.

FLORIZEL

> What, like a corpse?

PERDITA

> No, like a riverbank for love to lie and play on.
> Not like a corpse—or, if so, not one to be buried,
> but one alive and in my arms. Come, take your
> flowers. I think I am playing as I've seen them do
> during **Whitsun** festivities. This outfit I'm wearing
> certainly changes my attitude.

A religious feast celebrated seven Sundays after Easter.

FLORIZEL

> What you do is always better than what is normally
> done. When you speak, sweet, I'd have you do it
> forever. When you sing, I'd have you buy and sell
> with songs, and give alms, pray, and arrange your
> affairs with singing. When you dance, I wish you
> were a wave in the sea, so that you would only ever
> do that and have no other purpose in life. Everything
> you do is so perfect that whatever you do is the best.

PERDITA

> Oh, **Doricles**, you praise me too much. If your
> youth and your noble character didn't shine through
> your disguise and reveal your purity, I might worry
> that you were trying to lead me astray.

The fake name Florizel is using.

FLORIZEL

> I think you have as little cause to fear as I have intention
> to make you feel afraid. But come, dance with me please.
> Give me your hand, my Perdita, just as turtledoves pair
> for life and never part from one another.

PERDITA

180   I'll swear for 'em.

POLIXENES

This is the prettiest low-born lass that ever
Ran on the green-sward: nothing she does or seems
But smacks of something greater than herself,
Too noble for this place.

CAMILLO

185   He tells her something
That makes her blood look out: good sooth, she is
The queen of curds and cream.

CLOWN

                               Come on, strike up!

DORCAS

Mopsa must be your mistress: marry, garlic,
190   To mend her kissing with!

MOPSA

                            Now, in good time!

CLOWN

Not a word, a word; we stand upon our manners.
Come, strike up!

Music begins. Here a dance of Shepherds and Shepherdesses.

POLIXENES

Pray, good shepherd, what fair swain is this
195   Which dances with your daughter?

SHEPHERD

They call him Doricles; and boasts himself
To have a worthy feeding: but I have it
Upon his own report and I believe it;
He looks like sooth. He says he loves my daughter:
200   I think so too; for never gazed the moon
Upon the water as he'll stand and read
As 'twere my daughter's eyes: and, to be plain,
I think there is not half a kiss to choose
Who loves another best.

PERDITA

> I'll swear to their philosophy.

POLIXENES

> She is the prettiest common girl that's ever run across the lawn. Everything she does has an air of something greater than herself, something too noble for this place.

CAMILLO

> He's saying something that makes her blush. Goodness, her complexion is as creamy as milk.

YOKEL

> Come on, play the music!

DORCAS

> Mopsa will be your dance partner. Give her garlic to make her breath better!

MOPSA

> Now, that's enough!

YOKEL

> Don't say a word. We'll act with manners. Come, play the music!

Music plays. The shepherds and shepherdesses dance.

POLIXENES

> Good shepherd, can you tell me who is the handsome young man dancing with your daughter?

SHEPHERD

> They call him Doricles and say he has a valuable pasture. He's told me so himself, and I believe him. He looks honest. He says he loves my daughter, and I think he does. He gazes into my daughter's eyes as intently as the moon shines onto water. And, to be blunt, I don't think there's a way to tell from their kiss who loves the other more.

POLIXENES

205   She dances featly.

SHEPHERD

      So she does any thing; though I report it,
      That should be silent: if young Doricles
      Do light upon her, she shall bring him that
      Which he not dreams of.

Enter **SERVANT**

SERVANT

210   O master, if you did but hear the pedlar at the door, you
      would never dance again after a tabour and pipe; no, the
      bagpipe could not move you: he sings several tunes faster
      than you'll tell money; he utters them as he had eaten
      ballads and all men's ears grew to his tunes.

CLOWN

215   He could never come better; he shall come in. I love
      a ballad but even too well, if it be doleful matter
      merrily set down, or a very pleasant thing indeed and
      sung lamentably.

SERVANT

      He hath songs for man or woman, of all sizes; no milliner
220   can so fit his customers with gloves: he has the prettiest
      love-songs for maids; so without bawdry, which is strange;
      with such delicate burthens of dildos and fadings, 'jump
      her and thump her;' and where some stretch-mouthed
      rascal would, as it were, mean mischief and break a
225   foul gap into the matter, he makes the maid to answer
      'Whoop, do me no harm, good man;' puts him off, slights
      him, with 'Whoop, do me no harm, good man.'

POLIXENES

      This is a brave fellow.

CLOWN

      Believe me, thou talkest of an admirable conceited fellow.
230   Has he any unbraided wares?

POLIXENES

> She dances well.

SHEPHERD

> She does everything well. I'll tell you something I shouldn't: If young Doricles does marry her, she'll bring him greater fortune than he guesses.

A SERVANT enters.

SERVANT

> Oh, master, if you had heard the peddler at the door, you'd never again dance to a tambourine and a pipe, and a bagpipe wouldn't tempt you. He sings several songs faster than you can count money. He sings them as readily as if he had digested them completely, and all men can't help but listen.

YOKEL

> He couldn't have come at a better time. Let him in. I love a ballad almost too much, especially a sad subject set to a happy tune, or a pleasant subject sung mournfully.

SERVANT

> He has songs for all men and women. He fits them to his customers closer than gloves. He has pretty love songs for the maid, without any lewdness, which is unusual, and with **delicate refrains full of dildos and orgasms,** like "jump her and thump her." And if an obscene rascal would try to make mischief and interrupt the song, the peddler makes the maid answer, "Hey, do me no harm, good man," and puts him off that way.

The servant apparently doesn't understand that the songs are, in fact, full of sexual puns.

POLIXENES

> This is an excellent fellow.

YOKEL

> Believe me, you are talking about a very witty fellow. Does he have any new items to sell?

SERVANT

    He hath ribbons of an the colours i' the rainbow; points
    more than all the lawyers in Bohemia can learnedly
    handle, though they come to him by the gross: inkles,
    caddisses, cambrics, lawns: why, he sings 'em over as they
235   were gods or goddesses; you would think a smock were a
    she-angel, he so chants to the sleeve-hand and the work
    about the square on 't.

CLOWN

    Prithee bring him in; and let him approach singing.

PERDITA

    Forewarn him that he use no scurrilous words in 's tunes.

                             Exit SERVANT

CLOWN

240   You have of these pedlars, that have more in them than
    you'd think, sister.

PERDITA

    Ay, good brother, or go about to think.

    Enter AUTOLYCUS, *singing*

AUTOLYCUS

    Lawn as white as driven snow;
245   *Cyprus black as e'er was crow;*
    Gloves as sweet as damask roses;
    Masks for faces and for noses;
    Bugle bracelet, necklace amber,
    Perfume for a lady's chamber;
250   *Golden quoifs and stomachers,*
    For my lads to give their dears:
    Pins and poking-sticks of steel,
    What maids lack from head to heel:
    Come buy of me, come; come buy, come buy;
255   *Buy lads, or else your lasses cry: Come buy.*

SERVANT

> He has ribbons in all the colors of the rainbow, and countless laces that he gets wholesale. He has linen tape and yarn tape, fine linens, too. Why, he sings about them as if they were gods and goddesses. You would think a ladies' undergarment were an angel, the way he sings to the cuff and embroidery about the bodice.

YOKEL

> Please, let him in, and have him sing while he's approaching us.

PERDITA

> Warn him that he musn't use bad words in his songs.

> *The* SERVANT *exits.*

YOKEL

> There are some peddlers who have more bad words in them than you would think.

PERDITA

> Ay, good brother, or wish to think.

> AUTOLYCUS *enters, singing.*

AUTOLYCUS

> *Linen as white as wind-whipped snow;*
> **Crepe** *as black as a crow;*
> *Gloves as sweet-smelling as damask roses;*
> *Masks to cover faces and noses;*
> *A glittering bracelet, a necklace made of amber;*
> *Perfume made for a ladies' room;*
> *Golden caps and dress fronts*
> *For my young men to give to their sweethearts;*
> *Pins and rods of steel;*
> *Whatever young women need from head to toe;*
> *Come buy them from me, or your ladies will cry. Come buy.*

A material used for mourning clothes.

CLOWN

If I were not in love with Mopsa, thou shouldst take no
money of me; but being enthralled as I am, it will also be
the bondage of certain ribbons and gloves.

MOPSA

I was promised them against the feast; but they come not
260   too late now.

DORCAS

He hath promised you more than that, or there be liars.

MOPSA

He hath paid you all he promised you; may be, he has
paid you more, which will shame you to give him again.

CLOWN

Is there no manners left among maids? Will they wear
265   their plackets where they should bear their faces? Is
there not milking-time, when you are going to bed, or
kiln-hole, to whistle off these secrets, but you must be
tittle-tattling before all our guests? 'tis well they are
whispering: clamour your tongues, and not a word more.

MOPSA

270   I have done. Come, you promised me a tawdry-lace and a
pair of sweet gloves.

CLOWN

Have I not told thee how I was cozened by the way and
lost all my money?

AUTOLYCUS

And indeed, sir, there are cozeners abroad; therefore it
275   behoves men to be wary.

CLOWN

Fear not thou, man, thou shalt lose nothing here.

AUTOLYCUS

I hope so, sir; for I have about me many parcels of charge.

CLOWN

What hast here? ballads?

YOKEL

> If I weren't in love with Mopsa, I wouldn't give you a dime. But being infatuated as I am, I'll have to get a few ribbons and gloves.

MOPSA

> You promised them to me in time for the feast, but I guess it's not too late.

DORCAS

> He's promised more than that, or he is a liar.

MOPSA

> He has given you all he promised, and maybe a baby on top of it. It will shame you to pay him back with that baby in nine months.

YOKEL

> Don't you maids have any manners? Will you reveal your most intimate affairs in public? Isn't there a time to tell these secrets while you are milking, or going to bed, or at the fireplace, rather than tattling in front of our guests? Good thing they are whispering among themselves. Bite your tongues, and don't say another word.

MOPSA

> I won't. Come on, you promised me a cheap neckerchief and a pair of gloves.

YOKEL

> Didn't I tell you I was tricked along my way and lost all my money?

AUTOLYCUS

> It's true, sir. There are tricksters out there, so it's in a man's best interest to watch out.

YOKEL

> Don't fear, man, you won't lose anything here.

AUTOLYCUS

> I hope not, sir, since I have so many parcels of value.

YOKEL

> What do you have here? Ballads?

MOPSA

Pray now, buy some: I love a ballad in print o' life, for
280   then we are sure they are true.

AUTOLYCUS

Here's one to a very doleful tune, how a usurer's
wife was brought to bed of twenty money-bags at a
burthen and how she longed to eat adders' heads and
toads carbonadoed.

MOPSA

285   Is it true, think you?

AUTOLYCUS

Very true, and but a month old.

DORCAS

Bless me from marrying a usurer!

AUTOLYCUS

Here's the midwife's name to 't, one Mistress Tale-porter,
and five or six honest wives that were present. Why
290   should I carry lies abroad?

MOPSA

Pray you now, buy it.

CLOWN

Come on, lay it by: and let's first see more ballads; we'll
buy the other things anon.

AUTOLYCUS

Here's another ballad of a fish, that appeared upon
295   the coast on Wednesday the four-score of April, forty
thousand fathom above water, and sung this ballad
against the hard hearts of maids: it was thought she was a
woman and was turned into a cold fish for she would not
exchange flesh with one that loved her: the ballad is very
300   pitiful and as true.

DORCAS

Is it true too, think you?

AUTOLYCUS

Five justices' hands at it, and witnesses more than my
pack will hold.

MOPSA

> Please, buy some. I love having a ballad written out, because then we are sure it's true.

AUTOLYCUS

> Here's one that's sung to a very mournful tune: how a money lender's wife delivered twenty bags of money in one birth, and she wanted to eat snakes' heads and toads grilled.

MOPSA

> Do you think it's true?

AUTOLYCUS

> Very true, and only a month old.

DORCAS

> May I never marry a loan shark!

AUTOLYCUS

> Here's the name of the midwife who helped at the birth, one Mistress Tale-porter, and the five or six who witnessed it. Why should I spread lies around?

MOPSA

> Please, buy it.

YOKEL

> Come on, put it aside, and let's see more ballads before we buy anything.

AUTOLYCUS

> Here's another ballad about a fish that appeared on the shore on Wednesday, the eightieth of April, two hundred and forty thousand feet above sea level, and sang this song to soften the hearts of young women. Some thought it was a woman who had been changed into a cold fish because she wouldn't sleep with the man who loved her. The ballad is as sad as it is true.

DORCAS

> You think it's true, too?

AUTOLYCUS

> Five judges would swear to it, and there are more witnesses' statements than I could pack along with me.

CLOWN
>   Lay it by too: another.

AUTOLYCUS
305   This is a merry ballad, but a very pretty one.

MOPSA
>   Let's have some merry ones.

AUTOLYCUS
>   Why, this is a passing merry one and goes to the tune
>   of 'Two maids wooing a man:' there's scarce a maid
>   westward but she sings it; 'tis in request, I can tell you.

MOPSA
310   We can both sing it: if thou 'lt bear a part, thou shalt
>   hear; 'tis in three parts.

DORCAS
>   We had the tune on 't a month ago.

AUTOLYCUS
>   I can bear my part; you must know 'tis my occupation;
>   have at it with you.

Song

AUTOLYCUS
315   *Get you hence, for I must go*
>   *Where it fits not you to know.*

DORCAS
>   *Whither?*

MOPSA
>   *O, whither?*

DORCAS
>   *Whither?*

MOPSA
320   *It becomes thy oath full well,*
>   *Thou to me thy secrets tell.*

DORCAS
>   *Me too, let me go thither.*

YOKEL

> Put that one aside, too, and let's see another.

AUTOLYCUS

> This is a happy ballad, and very pretty.

MOPSA

> Let's have some happy ones.

AUTOLYCUS

> Here's a very merry one, which goes to the tune of "Two Maids Courting a Man." There's hardly a woman west of here that doesn't sing it. It's in great demand, I can tell you.

MOPSA

> We can both sing it. If you will sing one part, we can do it, since there are three parts and three of us.

DORCAS

> We learned the tune for it a month ago.

AUTOLYCUS

> I can sing my part. As you know, I'm a singer by trade. Go ahead.

They sing.

AUTOLYCUS

> *Go away, because I must go*
> *To a place that you don't know.*

DORCAS

> *Where?*

MOPSA

> *Oh, where?*

DORCAS

> *Where?*

MOPSA

> *It wouldn't be breaking your promise*
> *To tell me your secrets.*

DORCAS

> *Me, too, let me go with you.*

MOPSA

> Or thou goest to the grange or mill.

DORCAS

> If to either, thou dost ill.

AUTOLYCUS

325   Neither.

DORCAS

> What, neither?

AUTOLYCUS

> Neither.

DORCAS

> Thou hast sworn my love to be.

MOPSA

> Thou hast sworn it more to me:

330   Then whither goest? say, whither?

CLOWN

We'll have this song out anon by ourselves: my father and
the gentlemen are in sad talk, and we'll not trouble them.
Come, bring away thy pack after me. Wenches, I'll buy
for you both. Pedlar, let's have the first choice. Follow
335   me, girls.

Exeunt with DORCAS *and* MOPSA

AUTOLYCUS

And you shall pay well for 'em.
(Follows, singing:)
> Will you buy any tape,
> Or lace for your cape,
My dainty duck, my dear-a?
340   Any silk, any thread,
> Any toys for your head,
Of the new'st and finest, finest wear-a?
> Come to the pedlar;
> Money's a medler.
345   That doth utter all men's ware-a.

Exit

MOPSA

> Or perhaps you are going to the farmhouse or the mill.

DORCAS

> If you are going either place, you are doing wrong.

AUTOLYCUS

> I'm not going to either one.

DORCAS

> What, neither one?

AUTOLYCUS

> Neither one.

DORCAS

> You've sworn to be my love.

MOPSA

> You've sworn it more to me. Then where are you going?
>> Tell me, where?

YOKEL

We'll finish this song soon by ourselves. My father and the gentlemen are having a serious talk, and we should leave them alone. Come, bring your pack and follow me. Girls, I'll buy things for you both. Peddler, give me first choice. Follow me, girls.

> > > > > > *YOKEL, DORCAS, and MOPSA exit.*

AUTOLYCUS

And you will pay a great deal for them!
(he follows them, singing)
> Will you buy any ribbon,
> Or lace for your cape,
> My dainty little dear?
> Any silk, any thread,
> Any ornaments for your head,
> The newest and finest to wear?
> Come to the peddler
> Money is a meddler
> When it offers all a man's items for sale.

> > > > > > *He exits.*

Re-enter SERVANT

SERVANT

 Master, there is three carters, three shepherds, three neat-
 herds, three swine-herds, that have made themselves all
 men of hair, they call themselves Saltiers, and they have a
 dance which the wenches say is a gallimaufry of gambols,
350 because they are not in 't; but they themselves are o' the
 mind, if it be not too rough for some that know little but
 bowling, it will please plentifully.

SHEPHERD

 Away! we'll none on 't: here has been too much homely
 foolery already. I know, sir, we weary you.

POLIXENES

355 You weary those that refresh us: pray, let's see these four
 threes of herdsmen.

SERVANT

 One three of them, by their own report, sir, hath danced
 before the king; and not the worst of the three but jumps
 twelve foot and a half by the squier.

SHEPHERD

360 Leave your prating: since these good men are pleased, let
 them come in; but quickly now.

SERVANT

 Why, they stay at door, sir.

Exit

Here a dance of twelve Satyrs

POLIXENES

 O, father, you'll know more of that hereafter.
 (*to Camillo*) Is it not too far gone? 'Tis time to part them.
365 He's simple and tells much. (*to Florizel*) How now,
  fair shepherd!
 Your heart is full of something that does take

The SERVANT *re-enters.*

SERVANT
> Master, three cart drivers, three shepherds, three
> cowherds, and three swineherds have arrived, dressed
> up in animal skins. They call themselves jumpers,
> and they have a dance that the wenches say is filled
> with many leaps and hops. If it isn't too energetic for
> those more used to sedate sports like bowling, it will be
> greatly pleasing.

SHEPHERD
> Send them away! We'll have none of it. There has been
> too much vulgar foolishness already. I know, sir, that we
> are tiring you.

POLIXENES
> You'll tire those that entertain us. Please, let's see these
> four trios of herdsmen.

SERVANT
> One trio tells me that they have danced before the king.
> And even the worst of the three jumps twelve and half
> feet exactly.

SHEPHERD
> Stop your chattering. Since these good men would be
> pleased to see them, let them in, and quickly.

SERVANT
> Why, they're right at the door, sir.

He exits.

The twelve satyrs dance.

POLIXENES
> Oh, father, you'll know more about that soon.
> (*to Camillo*) Hasn't it gone too far? It's time to separate
> them. He's naïve and tells them too much. (*to Florizel*)
> Come now, handsome shepherd! There is something in
> your heart that is keeping your mind from enjoying the

Your mind from feasting. Sooth, when I was young
And handed love as you do, I was wont
370 To load my she with knacks: I would have ransack'd
The pedlar's silken treasury and have pour'd it
To her acceptance; you have let him go
And nothing marted with him. If your lass
Interpretation should abuse and call this
375 Your lack of love or bounty, you were straited
For a reply, at least if you make a care
Of happy holding her.

FLORIZEL

Old sir, I know
She prizes not such trifles as these are:
380 The gifts she looks from me are pack'd and lock'd
Up in my heart; which I have given already,
But not deliver'd. O, hear me breathe my life
Before this ancient sir, who, it should seem,
Hath sometime loved! I take thy hand, this hand,
385 As soft as dove's down and as white as it,
Or Ethiopian's tooth, or the fann'd snow that's bolted
By the northern blasts twice o'er.

POLIXENES

What follows this?
How prettily the young swain seems to wash
390 The hand was fair before! I have put you out:
But to your protestation; let me hear
What you profess.

FLORIZEL

Do, and be witness to 't.

POLIXENES

And this my neighbour too?

FLORIZEL

395 And he, and more
Than he, and men, the earth, the heavens, and all:
That, were I crown'd the most imperial monarch,
Thereof most worthy, were I the fairest youth

feast. When I was young and enjoyed love the way you do, I tended to give my girl lots of gifts. I would have ransacked the peddler's silks and treasures and given her them for her approval. You've let him go without buying a thing. If your lass interprets this as a lack of love or a lack of money, you'll have a hard time explaining it, at least if you want her to stay with you.

FLORIZEL

Old sir, I know she doesn't care for such trifles as these. The gifts she wants from me are from my heart, and they are hers already, though I haven't delivered them yet. (*to Perdita*) Oh, listen to me telling my private thoughts to this old man, who it seems has been in love on occasion! I take your hand, as soft and as white as a dove's downy feather, or the snow that is blown about by the wind.

POLIXENES

What does this mean? How delicately the young man seems to wash the hand that was already beautiful. I've interrupted. But back to your declaration. Let me hear more about your love.

FLORIZEL

Do, and witness how I feel.

POLIXENES

And my companion, too?

FLORIZEL

Him, and others, and all men, the Earth, the heavens and everything. If I were the most powerful and worthy king, or the most handsome youth to ever draw people's eyes, or if I had greater strength and knowledge than any other

That ever made eye swerve, had force and knowledge
400   More than was ever man's, I would not prize them
Without her love; for her employ them all;
Commend them and condemn them to her service
Or to their own perdition.

POLIXENES

Fairly offer'd.

CAMILLO

405   This shows a sound affection.

SHEPHERD

But, my daughter,
Say you the like to him?

PERDITA

I cannot speak
So well, nothing so well; no, nor mean better:
410   By the pattern of mine own thoughts I cut out
The purity of his.

SHEPHERD

Take hands, a bargain!
And, friends unknown, you shall bear witness to 't:
I give my daughter to him, and will make
415   Her portion equal his.

FLORIZEL

O, that must be
I' the virtue of your daughter: one being dead,
I shall have more than you can dream of yet;
Enough then for your wonder. But, come on,
420   Contract us 'fore these witnesses.

SHEPHERD

Come, your hand;
And, daughter, yours.

POLIXENES

Soft, swain, awhile, beseech you;
Have you a father?

FLORIZEL

425   I have: but what of him?

man, they would mean nothing to me without her love.
I would dedicate them to her service or sentence them
to damnation.

POLIXENES

Well said.

CAMILLO

This shows his strong affection for her.

SHEPHERD

But, my daughter, would you say the same to him?

PERDITA

I can't speak as well, not nearly as well. But I couldn't
say anything more. My own thoughts are echoed in his
pure words.

SHEPHERD

Shake hands. It's a deal! And, friendly strangers, you'll be
a witness to this. I give my daughter to him in marriage
and will make her dowry equal to his fortune.

FLORIZEL

Then her dowry must be her virtue, since once my father
is dead I will inherit more than you can dream of. It will
be enough for you to wonder at it. But, come, bind us
together before these witnesses.

SHEPHERD

Give me your hand, and daughter, give me yours.

POLIXENES

Gentle young shepherd, wait, please. Do you have
a father?

FLORIZEL

I do, but what about him?

POLIXENES

    Knows he of this?

FLORIZEL

                He neither does nor shall.

POLIXENES

    Methinks a father

    Is at the nuptial of his son a guest

430   That best becomes the table. Pray you once more,

    Is not your father grown incapable

    Of reasonable affairs? is he not stupid

    With age and altering rheums? can he speak? hear?

    Know man from man? dispute his own estate?

435   Lies he not bed-rid? and again does nothing

    But what he did being childish?

FLORIZEL

                   No, good sir;

    He has his health and ampler strength indeed

    Than most have of his age.

POLIXENES

440   By my white beard,

    You offer him, if this be so, a wrong

    Something unfilial: reason my son

    Should choose himself a wife, but as good reason

    The father, all whose joy is nothing else

445   But fair posterity, should hold some counsel

    In such a business.

FLORIZEL

               I yield all this;

    But for some other reasons, my grave sir,

    Which 'tis not fit you know, I not acquaint

450   My father of this business.

POLIXENES

                 Let him know 't.

FLORIZEL

    He shall not.

POLIXENES

Does he know about this?

FLORIZEL

He doesn't, and he won't.

POLIXENES

I think a father is the best guest at his son's wedding. Please, once more, has your father become incapable of doing normal tasks? Is he senile from age and illness? Can he speak and hear? Does he know one man from another? Can he handle his own estate? Is he confined to his bed and unable to do the things he did when he was younger?

FLORIZEL

No, good sir, he is healthy, and indeed he is even stronger than most people of his age.

POLIXENES

By my white beard, if this is so then you are wronging him in a way unsuitable for a son. It's reasonable that a son should choose a wife, but it's just as reasonable that his father should be able to have some say in the matter, since all his joy is in his family.

FLORIZEL

I agree with all you're saying. But there are other reasons, my serious sir, which it's best you don't know regarding why I don't tell my father of this.

POLIXENES

Let him know about it.

FLORIZEL

He won't know about it.

POLIXENES
                    Prithee, let him.

FLORIZEL
                              No, he must not.

SHEPHERD
455   Let him, my son: he shall not need to grieve
         At knowing of thy choice.

FLORIZEL
                                   Come, come, he must not.
         Mark our contract.

POLIXENES
                         Mark your divorce, young sir,
460   (*discovering himself*) Whom son I dare not call; thou art
                 too base
         To be acknowledged: thou a sceptre's heir,
         That thus affect'st a sheep-hook! (*to the Shepherd*)
                 Thou old traitor,
         I am sorry that by hanging thee I can
         But shorten thy life one week. (*to Perdita*) And thou,
                 fresh piece
465   Of excellent witchcraft, who of force must know
         The royal fool thou copest with,—

SHEPHERD
                              O, my heart!

POLIXENES
         I'll have thy beauty scratch'd with briers, and made
         More homely than thy state. For thee, fond boy,
470   If I may ever know thou dost but sigh
         That thou no more shalt see this knack, as never
         I mean thou shalt, we'll bar thee from succession;
         Not hold thee of our blood, no, not our kin,
         Far than Deucalion off: mark thou my words:
         Follow us to the court. Thou churl, for this time,
475   Though full of our displeasure, yet we free thee
         From the dead blow of it. And you, enchantment.—
         Worthy enough a herdsman: yea, him too,

POLIXENES

> Please, let him.

FLORIZEL

> No, he must not.

SHEPHERD

> Let him know, my son. He won't grieve when he hears your choice.

FLORIZEL

> Come, come, he must not know. Sign our contract.

POLIXENES

> Sign your divorce, young sir! (*he takes off his disguise*) I don't dare call you son. You are too lowly for me to acknowledge. You are the heir of a king, and you want to be a shepherd! (*to the Shepherd*) You old traitor, I'm sorry that hanging you will only shorten your life by a week! (*to Perdita*) And you, you skilled little witch, you must know you are dealing with a royal fool—

SHEPHERD

> Oh, my heart!

POLIXENES

> I'll have your beautiful face scratched with thorns and made worse than your social rank. (*to Florizel*) As for you, foolish boy, if I ever find out that you've so much as sighed about not seeing this whore again—as I mean you won't—I'll bar you from inheriting the throne. I won't consider you related to me at all. Listen to me: Follow me to the court, you delinquent, because this time I'll let you off easy, even though I am full of rage. (*to Perdita*) And you, witch, you're only good enough for a herdsman, and would be for Florizel, too, who lowers himself to the position of shepherd, if not for the royal blood in his

That makes himself, but for our honour therein,
Unworthy thee,—if ever henceforth thou
480   These rural latches to his entrance open,
Or hoop his body more with thy embraces,
I will devise a death as cruel for thee
As thou art tender to 't.

Exit

PERDITA
485   Even here undone!
I was not much afeard; for once or twice
I was about to speak and tell him plainly,
The selfsame sun that shines upon his court
Hides not his visage from our cottage but
490   Looks on alike. Will 't please you, sir, be gone?
I told you what would come of this: beseech you,
Of your own state take care: this dream of mine,—
Being now awake, I'll queen it no inch farther,
But milk my ewes and weep.

CAMILLO
495   Why, how now, father!
Speak ere thou diest.

SHEPHERD
                                    I cannot speak, nor think
Nor dare to know that which I know. O sir!
You have undone a man of fourscore three,
500   That thought to fill his grave in quiet, yea,
To die upon the bed my father died,
To lie close by his honest bones: but now
Some hangman must put on my shroud and lay me
Where no priest shovels in dust. O cursed wretch,
505   That knew'st this was the prince, and wouldst adventure
To mingle faith with him! Undone! undone!
If I might die within this hour, I have lived
To die when I desire.

Exit

veins. If you ever come near him or put your arms around him again, I'll devise a death for you that is as cruel as you are vulnerable to it.

He exits.

PERDITA

We're ruined even here! I was not very afraid. Once or twice I was about to speak and tell him bluntly that the same sun that illuminates his court doesn't hide its face from our cottage but looks down here all the same. Will you please leave, sir? I told you what would come of this. Please, take care of yourself. Now that I'm awake, I won't act the queen anymore but will milk my ewes and weep.

CAMILLO

Why, what about you, Father? Speak before you die.

SHEPHERD

I can't speak, or think, or dare to know what I know. Oh, sir! You have ruined a man of eighty-three. I thought I would go to my grave in peace, to die in the bed my father died in, and be buried close to his honest bones. But now a hangman will put a burial shroud on me and put me in an unconsecrated grave. (*to Perdita*) Oh, cursed girl, you knew this was the prince and dared to exchange vows with him! Undone! If I can die within the hour, I will have died when I wish.

He exits.

FLORIZEL

                      Why look you so upon me?
510   I am but sorry, not afeard; delay'd,
        But nothing alter'd: what I was, I am;
        More straining on for plucking back, not following
        My leash unwillingly.

CAMILLO

                      Gracious my lord,
515   You know your father's temper: at this time
        He will allow no speech, which I do guess
        You do not purpose to him; and as hardly
        Will he endure your sight as yet, I fear:
        Then, till the fury of his highness settle,
520   Come not before him.

FLORIZEL

                    I not purpose it.
        I think, Camillo?

CAMILLO

                Even he, my lord.

PERDITA

525   How often have I told you 'twould be thus!
        How often said, my dignity would last
        But till 'twere known!

FLORIZEL

                  It cannot fail but by
        The violation of my faith; and then
530   Let nature crush the sides o' the earth together
        And mar the seeds within! Lift up thy looks:
        From my succession wipe me, father; I
        Am heir to my affection.

CAMILLO

                Be advised.

FLORIZEL

535   I am, and by my fancy: if my reason
        Will thereto be obedient, I have reason;
        If not, my senses, better pleased with madness,
        Do bid it welcome.

FLORIZEL

> (*to Perdita*) Why do you look at me like that? I am only sorry, not afraid. Our plans are delayed, but not altered. I was in love, and I still am. Now I'm all the more determined to move forward for having been held back. I won't be pulled against my will.

CAMILLO

> My gracious lord, you know your father's temper. Just now he won't let you speak, which I guess you don't plan to do anyway, and I fear he can hardly stand to look at you yet. So, until his anger settles, don't approach him.

FLORIZEL

> I won't try it. Is it you, Camillo?

CAMILLO

> It is I, my lord.

PERDITA

> How often have I told you it would be this way! How often have I said that my dignity would only last as long as we weren't discovered!

FLORIZEL

> Your dignity will only be hurt if I break my promise to you, and if I do, may nature crush the Earth and any sources of life within it! Lift up your eyes. Let my father disown me as his heir. I am heir to my love.

CAMILLO

> Be careful.

FLORIZEL

> I am, by my heart. If my reason will obey love, I'll welcome reason. If not, I will be happier with madness and will welcome it gladly.

CAMILLO
                              This is desperate, sir.

FLORIZEL

540   So call it: but it does fulfil my vow;
        I needs must think it honesty. Camillo,
        Not for Bohemia, nor the pomp that may
        Be thereat glean'd, for all the sun sees or
        The close earth wombs or the profound sea hides
545   In unknown fathoms, will I break my oath
        To this my fair beloved: therefore, I pray you,
        As you have ever been my father's honour'd friend,
        When he shall miss me,—as, in faith, I mean not
        To see him any more,—cast your good counsels
550   Upon his passion; let myself and fortune
        Tug for the time to come. This you may know
        And so deliver, I am put to sea
        With her whom here I cannot hold on shore;
        And most opportune to our need I have
555   A vessel rides fast by, but not prepared
        For this design. What course I mean to hold
        Shall nothing benefit your knowledge, nor
        Concern me the reporting.

CAMILLO
                              O my lord!
560   I would your spirit were easier for advice,
        Or stronger for your need.

FLORIZEL
                              Hark, Perdita.
        (Drawing her aside) I'll hear you by and by.

CAMILLO
                              He's irremoveable,
565   Resolved for flight. Now were I happy, if
        His going I could frame to serve my turn,
        Save him from danger, do him love and honour,
        Purchase the sight again of dear Sicilia
        And that unhappy king, my master, whom
570   I so much thirst to see.

CAMILLO

> This is a desperate act, sir.

FLORIZEL

> You may call it that, but it does make good on what I just said, so I think it is an honest act. Camillo, I won't break my promise to Perdita for Bohemia, or all the glamour of being its king, or even for all the world the sun shines on, or the caves under the Earth, or the depths hidden by the sea. I don't mean to see my father again. So, please, as you have been his closest friend, speak wise words to him and soothe his anger when he realizes I'm gone. Let me wrestle with fortune for some time. You can tell my father that I've gone to sea with the woman I'm not allowed to hold on shore. Luckily for us, a vessel is close by, though it was not there for this purpose. It won't help either of us for me to tell you where we're going.

CAMILLO

> Oh, my lord! I wish you had a greater inclination to take advice, or that you were stronger.

FLORIZEL

> (*drawing Perdita aside*) Listen, Perdita. (*to Camillo*) Camillo, I'll listen to you in a moment.

CAMILLO

> He's made his mind up to flee. I would be happy if I could make this departure serve my own purposes. I can save him from danger and treat him with love and honor, and I can also gain sight of dear Sicilia and that unhappy king who is my master, and whom I long to see again.

FLORIZEL

Now, good Camillo;
I am so fraught with curious business that
I leave out ceremony.

CAMILLO

Sir, I think

575 You have heard of my poor services, i' the love
That I have borne your father?

FLORIZEL

Very nobly

Have you deserved: it is my father's music
To speak your deeds, not little of his care

580 To have them recompensed as thought on.

CAMILLO

Well, my lord,

If you may please to think I love the king
And through him what is nearest to him, which is
Your gracious self, embrace but my direction:

585 If your more ponderous and settled project
May suffer alteration, on mine honour,
I'll point you where you shall have such receiving
As shall become your highness; where you may
Enjoy your mistress, from the whom, I see,

590 There's no disjunction to be made, but by—
As heavens forefend!—your ruin; marry her,
And, with my best endeavours in your absence,
Your discontenting father strive to qualify
And bring him up to liking.

FLORIZEL

How, Camillo,

595 May this, almost a miracle, be done?
That I may call thee something more than man
And after that trust to thee.

CAMILLO

Have you thought on

600 A place whereto you'll go?

ORIGINAL TEXT

FLORIZEL

> Now, good Camillo, I'm so overwhelmed with this strange undertaking that I've forgotten my manners.

CAMILLO

> Sir, I think you have heard of the modest services and the love I have given your father?

FLORIZEL

> The praise is well-deserved. My father delights to speak of your actions, and he hopes that he repays them as much as he praises them.

CAMILLO

> Well, my lord, if you do believe that I love the king and what he holds most dear, which is you, take my advice: If your determined course might be altered a bit, I swear I'll show you a place where you'll be received in a manner fit for your highness. There you'll be able to enjoy life with your sweetheart, from whom I can see there is no chance of separating you except—heaven forbid!—through your ruin. Marry her, and I'll strive in your absence to talk down your unhappy father and turn him to approval.

FLORIZEL

> How might this near miracle be accomplished, Camillo? If you can do it, I would say you're something more than a man and would always trust you.

CAMILLO

> Have you thought about where you'll go?

FLORIZEL

Not any yet:
But as the unthought-on accident is guilty
To what we wildly do, so we profess
Ourselves to be the slaves of chance and flies
605   Of every wind that blows.

CAMILLO

Then list to me:
This follows, if you will not change your purpose
But undergo this flight, make for Sicilia,
And there present yourself and your fair princess,
610   For so I see she must be, 'fore Leontes:
She shall be habited as it becomes
The partner of your bed. Methinks I see
Leontes opening his free arms and weeping
His welcomes forth; asks thee the son forgiveness,
615   As 'twere i' the father's person; kisses the hands
Of your fresh princess; o'er and o'er divides him
'Twixt his unkindness and his kindness; the one
He chides to hell and bids the other grow
Faster than thought or time.

FLORIZEL

620   Worthy Camillo,
What colour for my visitation shall I
Hold up before him?

CAMILLO

Sent by the king your father
To greet him and to give him comforts. Sir,
625   The manner of your bearing towards him, with
What you as from your father shall deliver,
Things known betwixt us three, I'll write you down:
The which shall point you forth at every sitting
What you must say; that he shall not perceive
630   But that you have your father's bosom there
And speak his very heart.

FLORIZEL

> Not any place yet. But since an unforeseen accident
> caused us to take this course of action, we'll pledge
> ourselves to fate and go where the wind blows us.

CAMILLO

> Then listen to me. If you won't change your mind and are
> determined to flee, head to Sicilia, and present yourself
> and your fair princess before Leontes. She should be
> dressed in a way suitable for the wife of a prince. I think
> Leontes will open his arms and will weep as he bids you
> welcome. He'll ask your forgiveness as though he were
> your father, and he'll kiss your princess's hands. He's
> caught between berating himself for his past unkindness
> to your father and trying to be more kind now.

FLORIZEL

> Worthy Camillo, what reason should I give him for
> my visit?

CAMILLO

> Tell him you are sent by your father to greet him and
> comfort him. I'll write you a note containing things
> known by the three of us telling you what to say. That
> and the manner with which you greet him will make him
> believe that you represent your father's feelings.

FLORIZEL

                  I am bound to you:
There is some sap in this.

CAMILLO

                  A course more promising

635   Than a wild dedication of yourselves
To unpath'd waters, undream'd shores, most certain
To miseries enough; no hope to help you,
But as you shake off one to take another;
Nothing so certain as your anchors, who
Do their best office, if they can but stay you

640   Where you'll be loath to be: besides you know
Prosperity's the very bond of love,
Whose fresh complexion and whose heart together
Affliction alters.

PERDITA

             One of these is true:

645   I think affliction may subdue the cheek,
But not take in the mind.

CAMILLO

            Yea, say you so?
There shall not at your father's house these seven years
Be born another such.

FLORIZEL

650   My good Camillo,
She is as forward of her breeding as
She is i' the rear our birth.

CAMILLO

          I cannot say 'tis pity
She lacks instructions, for she seems a mistress

655   To most that teach.

PERDITA

        Your pardon, sir; for this
I'll blush you thanks.

FLORIZEL

> I owe you for this. There's life in this plan.

CAMILLO

> It's a much more promising way of doing things than simply throwing yourself on unmarked waters and strange shores, which will certainly lead you to plenty of misery. There would be no hope to help you, aside from casting off one shore to find another. Your anchors would be your only certainty, and the best they can do is hold you in a place you'll be loath to remain. Besides, you know that good fortune keeps love strong, and that affliction will change the freshness of your affection and the feelings of your heart.

PERDITA

> One of those is true. Affliction may make us less fresh, but it won't alter our feelings.

CAMILLO

> Do you say so? There won't be anyone like you born at your father's house for many years.

FLORIZEL

> My good Camillo, she is as superior to her upbringing as she is inferior to our noble rank.

CAMILLO

> I can't say it's a pity she's uneducated, because she seems more intelligent than those that teach.

PERDITA

> Pardon me, sir, I'll thank you with my blushing.

FLORIZEL

My prettiest Perdita!
But O, the thorns we stand upon! Camillo,
Preserver of my father, now of me,
660   The medicine of our house, how shall we do?
We are not furnish'd like Bohemia's son,
Nor shall appear in Sicilia.

CAMILLO

My lord,
Fear none of this: I think you know my fortunes
665   Do all lie there: it shall be so my care
To have you royally appointed as if
The scene you play were mine. For instance, sir,
That you may know you shall not want, one word.

They talk aside

Re-enter **AUTOLYCUS**

AUTOLYCUS

Ha, ha! what a fool Honesty is! and Trust, his sworn
670   brother, a very simple gentleman! I have sold all my
trumpery; not a counterfeit stone, not a ribbon, glass,
pomander, brooch, table-book, ballad, knife, tape,
glove, shoe-tie, bracelet, horn-ring, to keep my pack
from fasting: they throng who should buy first, as if my
675   trinkets had been hallowed and brought a benediction to
the buyer: by which means I saw whose purse was best in
picture; and what I saw, to my good use I remembered.
My clown, who wants but something to be a reasonable
man, grew so in love with the wenches' song, that he
680   would not stir his pettitoes till he had both tune and
words; which so drew the rest of the herd to me that all
their other senses stuck in ears: you might have pinched a
placket, it was senseless; 'twas nothing to geld a codpiece
of a purse; I could have filed keys off that hung in chains:
685   no hearing, no feeling, but my sir's song, and admiring

FLORIZEL

My pretty Perdita! But, oh, the danger we're in! Camillo, you've rescued my father and now me. You heal our family. What will we do? I'm not dressed like the king's son, and I certainly won't look like royalty once we reach Sicilia.

CAMILLO

My lord, don't worry about it. I think you know that my fortune is still in Sicilia. I'll make sure you are dressed as royally as if I were dressing you for a play I had written. Let me have a word with you, to reassure you that you won't be left in need.

They talk off to the side.

AUTOLYCUS *re-enters.*

AUTOLYCUS

Ha-ha! Honesty is such a fool, and Trust, his brother, is so naïve! I have sold all my goods—not a fake stone, or a ribbon, glass, brooch, book, ballad, knife, tape, glove, shoelace, bracelet, or ring made of horn remains in my pack. They crowded around me to see who could buy first, as if my trinkets were blessed and brought grace to the buyer. It let me know who had the fullest purse, and what I saw I remembered to put to use later. The yokel, who lacks just one quality to be a reasonable man, loved the girls' song so much that he wouldn't leave until he had bought both the tune and the words. And all the others were so entranced that it was as though all their other senses were committed to hearing. You could have stolen a skirt because no one could feel anything. It was easy to strip a purse from a **codpiece**, and I could have used a file to take keys

Part of a man's clothing attached to the front of his hose and covering his genitals.

the nothing of it. So that in this time of lethargy I picked
and cut most of their festival purses; and had not the old
man come in with a whoo-bub against his daughter and
the king's son and scared my choughs from the chaff, I
690   had not left a purse alive in the whole army.

CAMILLO, FLORIZEL, *and* PERDITA *come forward*

CAMILLO

Nay, but my letters, by this means being there
So soon as you arrive, shall clear that doubt.

FLORIZEL

And those that you'll procure from King Leontes—

CAMILLO

Shall satisfy your father.

PERDITA

695   Happy be you!
All that you speak shows fair.

CAMILLO

(Seeing AUTOLYCUS*)*   Who have we here?
We'll make an instrument of this, omit
Nothing may give us aid.

AUTOLYCUS

700   If they have overheard me now, why, hanging.

CAMILLO

How now, good fellow! why shakest thou so? Fear
not, man; here's no harm intended to thee.

AUTOLYCUS

I am a poor fellow, sir.

CAMILLO

Why, be so still; here's nobody will steal that from thee:
705   yet for the outside of thy poverty we must make an
exchange; therefore discase thee instantly, —thou must
think there's a necessity in 't,—and change garments with
this gentleman: though the pennyworth on his side be the
worst, yet hold thee, there's some boot.

off a chain. There was no hearing or feeling anything
except for that song, and admiration for it. So while
they were spellbound I stole most of their purses,
which were filled with money for the festival. If the
old man hadn't come in wailing about his daughter
and the king's son and scared my little birds from the
feed, I would have taken purses from everyone.

CAMILLO, FLORIZEL, *and* PERDITA *approach.*

CAMILLO

No, but my letters will be there as soon as you arrive, and
they'll clear up that question.

FLORIZEL

And the letter that you'll get from King Leontes—

CAMILLO

Will set your father at ease.

PERDITA

May you be happy! All your plans are good.

CAMILLO

Who is this? (*seeing Autolycus*) We'll use this man, since
we should use anything that will help.

AUTOLYCUS

If they've overheard me, I'll be hanged.

CAMILLO

How are you, good fellow? Why are you shaking? Don't
worry, man, we don't intend you any harm.

AUTOLYCUS

I am a poor man, sir.

CAMILLO

Why, be still. No one here will steal from you. But we
need your poor-looking clothes. Undress right now—it's
urgent—and swap clothes with this gentleman. The
bargain is bad for him, but wait, (*giving him money*)
there's something more in it for you.

AUTOLYCUS

710   I am a poor fellow, sir. (*aside*) I know ye well enough.

CAMILLO

Nay, prithee, dispatch: the gentleman is half
flayed already.

AUTOLYCUS

Are you in earnest, sir? (*aside*) I smell the trick on 't.

FLORIZEL

Dispatch, I prithee.

AUTOLYCUS

715   Indeed, I have had earnest: but I cannot with conscience
take it.

CAMILLO

Unbuckle, unbuckle.

FLORIZEL *and* **AUTOLYCUS** *exchange garments*

Fortunate mistress,—let my prophecy
Come home to ye!—you must retire yourself
720   Into some covert: take your sweetheart's hat
And pluck it o'er your brows, muffle your face,
Dismantle you, and, as you can, disliken
The truth of your own seeming; that you may—
For I do fear eyes over—to shipboard
725   Get undescried.

PERDITA

                I see the play so lies
That I must bear a part.

CAMILLO

                No remedy.
Have you done there?

FLORIZEL

730   Should I now meet my father,
He would not call me son.

AUTOLYCUS

> I am a poor man, sir. (*aside*) I know you well enough.

CAMILLO

> No, please, hurry. The gentleman is already
> half undressed.

AUTOLYCUS

> Are you serious, sir? (*aside*) I think it's a trick.

FLORIZEL

> Hurry, I beg you.

AUTOLYCUS

> Indeed, I think it is sincere, but I can't believe it.

CAMILLO

> Unbuckle, unbuckle.

> FLORIZEL *and* AUTOLYCUS *exchange clothing.*

> (*to Perdita*) Lucky mistress—may you be lucky yet! You
> must take a disguise. Put on your sweetheart's hat and
> pull it down over your eyes, wrap up your face, take off
> your outer garments, and, as much as you can, change
> your appearance as much as possible. That way I hope
> you'll get to the ship without being discovered, for I fear
> that people are watching for you.

PERDITA

> I understand that what we're doing means I have to play
> a role.

CAMILLO

> There's no helping it. Are you done there?

FLORIZEL

> If I ran into my father now, he wouldn't know me as
> his son.

CAMILLO

     Nay, you shall have no hat. *(Giving it to* PERDITA*)*
Come, lady, come. Farewell, my friend.

AUTOLYCUS

           Adieu, sir.

FLORIZEL

735 O Perdita, what have we twain forgot!
Pray you, a word.

CAMILLO

(aside) What I do next, shall be to tell the king
Of this escape and whither they are bound;
Wherein my hope is I shall so prevail
To force him after: in whose company
740 I shall review Sicilia, for whose sight
I have a woman's longing.

FLORIZEL

        Fortune speed us!
Thus we set on, Camillo, to the sea-side.

CAMILLO

The swifter speed the better.

      Exeunt FLORIZEL, PERDITA, *and* CAMILLO

AUTOLYCUS

745 I understand the business, I hear it: to have an open
ear, a quick eye, and a nimble hand, is necessary for
a cut-purse; a good nose is requisite also, to smell out
work for the other senses. I see this is the time that the
unjust man doth thrive. What an exchange had this been
750 without boot! What a boot is here with this exchange!
Sure the gods do this year connive at us, and we may
do any thing extempore. The prince himself is about a
piece of iniquity, stealing away from his father with his
clog at his heels: if I thought it were a piece of honesty to
755 acquaint the king withal, I would not do 't: I hold it the
more knavery to conceal it; and therein am I constant to
my profession.

CAMILLO

> No, you won't have a hat. (*he gives it to* Perdita) Come along, lady, come. Farewell, my friend.

AUTOLYCUS

> Goodbye, sir.

FLORIZEL

> Oh, Perdita, we've forgotten something now! Please, let's have a word.

CAMILLO

> (*aside*) Next I'll tell the king that they've escaped and where they are going. Then I hope I can persuade him to follow after them, and in his company I'll then return to Sicilia, which I've longed to see again.

FLORIZEL

> May fortune speed us! So we set forth to sea, Camillo.

CAMILLO

> The faster the better.

> FLORIZEL, PERDITA, *and* CAMILLO *exit*.

AUTOLYCUS

> I think I understand this matter and am hearing it right. It's necessary for a thief to have an open ear, a quick eye, and a nimble hand. A good nose is needed, too, to find work for the other senses. I see that this is a time when the unfair man thrives. What an exchange this would have been even without payment! What a profit I got through this exchange! Surely the gods are indulging us, and we can do whatever we want on a whim. The prince himself is doing wrong, sneaking away from his father with his girlfriend. If I thought it were an honest deed to tell the king, I wouldn't do it. I think it is more dishonest to conceal it, so I'll remain true to my profession and say nothing.

Re-enter CLOWN *and* SHEPHERD

Aside, aside; here is more matter for a hot brain: every
lane's end, every shop, church, session, hanging, yields a
760   careful man work.

CLOWN

See, see; what a man you are now!
There is no other way but to tell the king she's a
changeling and none of your flesh and blood.

SHEPHERD

Nay, but hear me.

CLOWN

765   Nay, but hear me.

SHEPHERD

Go to, then.

CLOWN

She being none of your flesh and blood, your flesh and
blood has not offended the king; and so your flesh and
blood is not to be punished by him. Show those things
770   you found about her, those secret things, all but what
she has with her: this being done, let the law go whistle: I
warrant you.

SHEPHERD

I will tell the king all, every word, yea, and his son's
pranks too; who, I may say, is no honest man, neither to
775   his father nor to me, to go about to make me the king's
brother-in-law.

CLOWN

Indeed, brother-in-law was the farthest off you could
have been to him and then your blood had been the
dearer by I know how much an ounce.

AUTOLYCUS

780   (*aside*) Very wisely, puppies!

SHEPHERD

Well, let us to the king: there is that in this fardel will
make him scratch his beard.

The YOKEL *and the* SHEPHERD *re-enter.*

Aha, here is more to do for a sharp mind. Every lane,
every shop, church, meeting, or hanging gives a careful
man an opportunity.

YOKEL

See, look at the situation you are in now! There's no
way out but to tell the king that she's a **changeling**
and not your flesh and blood.

> A child believed
> to have been
> secretly swapped
> for the parents'
> real child by
> fairies.

SHEPHERD

Perhaps, but listen to me.

YOKEL

No, listen to me.

SHEPHERD

Go on, then.

YOKEL

Since she's not actually related to you, your family hasn't
offended the king, and so he shouldn't punish your
family. Show him what secret things you've found with
her, everything but what she has on her. Once that's
done, the law will have nothing on you, I guarantee you.

SHEPHERD

I'll tell the king everything, yes, every word, and I'll
reveal his son's pranks, too. I must say, his son isn't an
honest man to either his father or to me, trying to make
me the king's brother-in-law.

YOKEL

Indeed, brother-in-law is the furthest you could be
from him, and your blood would have been not at all
more valuable.

AUTOLYCUS

(*aside*) Very wise, gullible men!

SHEPHERD

Well, let's go to the king. There is something in this
bundle that will make him reconsider things.

AUTOLYCUS

(*aside*) I know not what impediment this complaint may
be to the flight of my master.

CLOWN

785 Pray heartily he be at palace.

AUTOLYCUS

(*aside*) Though I am not naturally honest, I am so
sometimes by chance: let me pocket up my pedlar's
excrement. (*takes off his false beard*) How now, rustics!
whither are you bound?

SHEPHERD

790 To the palace, an it like your worship.

AUTOLYCUS

Your affairs there, what, with whom, the condition of that
fardel, the place of your dwelling, your names, your ages,
of what having, breeding, and any thing that is fitting to
be known, discover.

CLOWN

795 We are but plain fellows, sir.

AUTOLYCUS

A lie; you are rough and hairy. Let me have no lying:
it becomes none but tradesmen, and they often give us
soldiers the lie: but we pay them for it with stamped coin,
not stabbing steel; therefore they do not give us the lie.

CLOWN

800 Your worship had like to have given us one, if you had not
taken yourself with the manner.

SHEPHERD

Are you a courtier, an 't like you, sir?

AUTOLYCUS

Whether it like me or no, I am a courtier. Seest thou
not the air of the court in these enfoldings? hath not
805 my gait in it the measure of the court? receives not thy
nose court-odor from me? reflect I not on thy baseness
court-contempt? Thinkest thou, for that I insinuate, or

AUTOLYCUS

> (*aside*) I don't know how this complaint might hinder the flight of Florizel, my master.

YOKEL

> Let's hope that he's at the palace.

AUTOLYCUS

> (*aside*) Even if I'm not naturally honest, sometimes I happen to be. Let me take off my peddler's beard. *(He takes off his false beard.)* Hello, countrymen! Where are you going?

SHEPHERD

> To the palace, if it pleases your worship.

AUTOLYCUS

> Tell me what your business is there, and with whom, what's in that bundle, where you live, your names, ages, what you own and your parents, or anything else that ought to be known.

YOKEL

> We're just ordinary fellows, sir.

AUTOLYCUS

> That's a lie. You're ragged-looking and hairy. Don't lie to me. It only works for tradesmen, and they often call us soldiers liars and cheat us at the same time. But we pay them for it with coins rather than swords, so they're not really giving us lies since we're paying.

YOKEL

> You would have given us a lie if you hadn't stopped yourself in the middle.

SHEPHERD

> Are you from the court, if you please, sir?

AUTOLYCUS

> I am from the court, whether it please me or not. Don't you see an air of the court in my clothes? Don't I walk as though I'm from the court? Don't you smell the odor of the court on me? Don't I treat your base rank with the contempt of the court? Do you think that because I subtly

toze from thee thy business, I am therefore no courtier?
I am courtier cap-a-pe; and one that will either push on
810 or pluck back thy business there: whereupon I command
thee to open thy affair.

SHEPHERD

My business, sir, is to the king.

AUTOLYCUS

What advocate hast thou to him?

SHEPHERD

I know not, an 't like you.

CLOWN

815 Advocate's the court-word for a pheasant: say you
have none.

SHEPHERD

None, sir; I have no pheasant, cock nor hen.

AUTOLYCUS

How blessed are we that are not simple men!
Yet nature might have made me as these are,
820 Therefore I will not disdain.

CLOWN

This cannot be but a great courtier.

SHEPHERD

His garments are rich, but he wears them
not handsomely.

CLOWN

He seems to be the more noble in being fantastical: a
825 great man, I'll warrant; I know by the picking on 's teeth.

AUTOLYCUS

The fardel there? what's i' the fardel?
Wherefore that box?

SHEPHERD

Sir, there lies such secrets in this fardel and box, which
none must know but the king; and which he shall know
830 within this hour, if I may come to the speech of him.

draw out your business from you, that I'm not from the court? I am a courtier from head to foot. And I'll either push along or prevent your business there, so I command you to tell me what it's about.

SHEPHERD

My business, sir, is with the king.

AUTOLYCUS

Do you have an advocate with him?

SHEPHERD

I don't know.

YOKEL

An **advocate means a pheasant at the court**; say you don't have one.

The Yokel thinks advocate means "bribe," and game birds like pheasants were supposedly given as bribes at local courts.

SHEPHERD

None, sir. I don't have a pheasant, either a male or a female one.

AUTOLYCUS

How blessed are we that are smart! Yet nature could have made me just like them, so I won't treat them with contempt.

YOKEL

He must be a great man at the court.

SHEPHERD

His garments look expensive, but he doesn't wear them well.

YOKEL

His oddness makes him seem even more noble. I'll bet that he's a great man. I know by the **toothpicks he uses**.

Ornate toothpicks were fashionable at the time.

AUTOLYCUS

What about that bundle there? What is in the bundle? And in the box?

SHEPHERD

Sir, the bundle and the box hold secrets that only the king may know, and which he'll know within the hour if I can speak to him.

AUTOLYCUS

Age, thou hast lost thy labour.

SHEPHERD

Why, sir?

AUTOLYCUS

The king is not at the palace; he is gone aboard a new ship
to purge melancholy and air himself: for, if thou beest
835   capable of things serious, thou must know the king is full
of grief.

SHEPHERD

So 'tis said, sir; about his son, that should have married a
shepherd's daughter.

AUTOLYCUS

If that shepherd be not in hand-fast, let him fly: the
840   curses he shall have, the tortures he shall feel, will break
the back of man, the heart of monster.

CLOWN

Think you so, sir?

AUTOLYCUS

Not he alone shall suffer what wit can make heavy
and vengeance bitter; but those that are germane to
him, though removed fifty times, shall all come under
845   the hangman: which though it be great pity, yet it is
necessary. An old sheep-whistling rogue a ram-tender,
to offer to have his daughter come into grace! Some say
he shall be stoned; but that death is too soft for him, say I
draw our throne into a sheep-cote! all deaths are too few,
850   the sharpest too easy.

CLOWN

Has the old man e'er a son, sir, do you hear, an 't like
you, sir?

AUTOLYCUS

He has a son, who shall be flayed alive; then 'nointed over
with honey, set on the head of a wasp's nest; then stand
855   till he be three quarters and a dram dead; then recovered

AUTOLYCUS

> Old man, you have wasted your work.

SHEPHERD

> Why, sir?

AUTOLYCUS

> The king isn't at the palace. He's gone on a new ship to ease his sadness and to refresh himself. If you are able to grasp such serious things, you know that the king is full of grief.

SHEPHERD

> So it is said, sir, because his son meant to marry a shepherd's daughter.

AUTOLYCUS

> If the shepherd hasn't been arrested already, he should flee. He'll suffer curses so fierce and tortures so terrible that it would break the back of a man and the heart of even a monster.

YOKEL

> Do you think so, sir?

AUTOLYCUS

> He won't suffer these harsh and bitter punishments alone, either. All those who are related to him, even if they are very distant relatives, will hang, too. It's a great pity, but it's necessary. That an old shepherd and rogue would act as a broker and offer to have his daughter marry into the royal family! Some say he'll be stoned, but that manner of death is too soft for someone who tried to drag the throne into a sheep's pen! He can't die too many times, or in too painful a way.

YOKEL

> Have you heard if the old man has a son?

AUTOLYCUS

> He has a son who will be whipped, then covered with honey and put on a wasp's nest until he is three quarters of the way to death. Then he'll be revived with liquor

again with aqua-vitae or some other hot infusion; then,
raw as he is, and in the hottest day prognostication
proclaims, shall he be set against a brick-wall, the sun
looking with a southward eye upon him, where he is to
860   behold him with flies blown to death. But what talk we
of these traitorly rascals, whose miseries are to be smiled
at, their offences being so capital? Tell me, for you seem
to be honest plain men, what you have to the king: being
something gently considered, I'll bring you where he is
865   aboard, tender your persons to his presence, whisper him
in your behalfs; and if it be in man besides the king to
effect your suits, here is man shall do it.

CLOWN

He seems to be of great authority: close with him, give
him gold; and though authority be a stubborn bear, yet
870   he is oft led by the nose with gold: show the inside of
your purse to the outside of his hand, and no more ado.
Remember 'stoned,' and 'flayed alive.'

SHEPHERD

An 't please you, sir, to undertake the business for us,
here is that gold I have: I'll make it as much more and
875   leave this young man in pawn till I bring it you.

AUTOLYCUS

After I have done what I promised?

SHEPHERD

Ay, sir.

AUTOLYCUS

Well, give me the moiety. Are you a party in
this business?

CLOWN

880   In some sort, sir: but though my case be a pitiful one, I
hope I shall not be flayed out of it.

AUTOLYCUS

O, that's the case of the shepherd's son: hang him, he'll
be made an example.

or some other hot drink. Then, raw as his flesh is, on
the hottest day that can be predicted he'll be set against
a brick wall with the sun beating down upon him, and
where he will be swarmed with flies. But why are we
talking about these traitors, whose offenses are so terrible
that their misery should cause us happiness? Tell me,
since you seem to be honest, ordinary men, what business
do you have with the king? Since I'm well respected
at court, I'll take you to his ship, bring you into his
presence, and whisper to him a recommendation on your
behalf. If there is any man beside the king who can help
your case, that's me.

YOKEL

He seems to have a great deal of authority. Approach him
and give him some money. No matter how stubborn and
untamable authority may be, a little money can make
him docile. Let him put his hand into your purse, and no
more fuss. Remember: "stoned," and "flayed alive."

SHEPHERD

If it pleases you, sir, to take on this business for us, here
is all the gold I have. I'll pay you an equal amount more,
and I'll leave you this young man as a guarantee until I
can bring the rest to you.

AUTOLYCUS

After I have done what I have promised?

SHEPHERD

Yes, sir.

AUTOLYCUS

Well then, give me the first half. Are you part of
this deal?

YOKEL

In a way, sir. But even if my skin is pitiful, I hope I won't
be whipped out of it.

AUTOLYCUS

Oh no, that's what will happen to the shepherd's son.
He'll be hanged as an example.

CLOWN

885 Comfort, good comfort! We must to the king and show
our strange sights: he must know 'tis none of your
daughter nor my sister; we are gone else. Sir, I will give
you as much as this old man does when the business is
performed, and remain, as he says, your pawn till it be
brought you.

AUTOLYCUS

890 I will trust you. Walk before toward the sea-side; go
on the right hand: I will but look upon the hedge and
follow you.

CLOWN

We are blest in this man, as I may say, even blest.

SHEPHERD

Let's before as he bids us: he was provided to do us good.

Exeunt SHEPHERD *and* CLOWN

AUTOLYCUS

895 If I had a mind to be honest, I see Fortune would not
suffer me: she drops booties in my mouth. I am courted
now with a double occasion, gold and a means to do the
prince my master good; which who knows how that may
turn back to my advancement? I will bring these two
900 moles, these blind ones, aboard him: if he think it fit to
shore them again and that the complaint they have to
the king concerns him nothing, let him call me rogue for
being so far officious; for I am proof against that title and
what shame else belongs to 't. To him will I present them:
905 there may be matter in it.

Exit

YOKEL

(to the Shepherd) What a comfort! We must go to the king and show him our amazing proof. He must know that Perdita isn't your daughter or my sister, or we'll be dead. (to Autolycus) Sir, I will give you as much money as this old man does once the business is concluded, and until then, I'll stay with you as a guarantee for payment.

AUTOLYCUS

I trust you. Walk straight ahead toward the sea. Go along the right-hand side of the road. I just need to go to the bathroom and I'll follow you.

YOKEL

We're blessed to have this man with us, I say, blessed.

SHEPHERD

Let's go before he has to tell us again. He was put here to help us.

The **SHEPHERD** *and the* **YOKEL** *exit.*

AUTOLYCUS

Even if I wanted to be honest, I see Fate wouldn't let me. She drops profits right in my pocket. I have two opportunities here: to get gold and to do something good for my master the prince—and who knows how that will help me in the future. I will bring these two gullible men aboard the ship with him. If he thinks their complaint to the king has nothing to do with him and wants to put them back on shore again, let him call me a rogue for being so interfering. I can't be hurt by that name, or any shame attached to it. I'll present them to him. There might be money in it.

He exits.

ACT FIVE
SCENE 1

A room in LEONTES' *palace.*
Enter LEONTES, CLEOMENES, DION, PAULINA, *and* SERVANTS

CLEOMENES
> Sir, you have done enough, and have perform'd
> A saint-like sorrow: no fault could you make,
> Which you have not redeem'd; indeed, paid down
> More penitence than done trespass: at the last,
> 5   Do as the heavens have done, forget your evil;
> With them forgive yourself.

LEONTES
>   Whilst I remember
> Her and her virtues, I cannot forget
> My blemishes in them, and so still think of
> 10   The wrong I did myself; which was so much,
> That heirless it hath made my kingdom and
> Destroy'd the sweet'st companion that e'er man
> Bred his hopes out of.

PAULINA
>   True, too true, my lord:
> 15   If, one by one, you wedded all the world,
> Or from the all that are took something good,
> To make a perfect woman, she you kill'd
> Would be unparallel'd.

LEONTES
>   I think so. Kill'd!
> 20   She I kill'd! I did so: but thou strikest me
> Sorely, to say I did; it is as bitter
> Upon thy tongue as in my thought: now, good now,
> Say so but seldom.

ACT FIVE
SCENE 1

A room in LEONTES's *palace.*
LEONTES, CLEOMENES, DION, PAULINA, *and several Servants enter.*

CLEOMENES

(*to Leontes*) Sir, you have done enough and have shown the sorrow and piety of a saint. You have redeemed every mistake you might have made, and have paid more penance than you have done wrong. At last, forgive your sins as Heaven has forgiven it, and forgive yourself.

LEONTES

As long as I remember her and her virtue, I can't forget how I attacked them, and I still think of the wrong I did. My misbehavior was so terrible that it has left my kingdom without an heir and destroyed the sweetest companion that a man could hope would bear his children.

PAULINA

It is too true, my lord. Even if you wedded every woman in the world one by one, or took the best quality from each and made the perfect woman, the woman you killed couldn't be matched.

LEONTES

I think so, too. Killed! The woman I killed! I did, but you wound me deeply to say it so bluntly. You say it as bitterly as I think it. Now, please, don't say it often.

CLEOMENES
                    Not at all, good lady:
25   You might have spoken a thousand things that would
      Have done the time more benefit and graced
      Your kindness better.

PAULINA
                              You are one of those
      Would have him wed again.

DION
30   If you would not so,
      You pity not the state, nor the remembrance
      Of his most sovereign name; consider little
      What dangers, by his highness' fail of issue,
      May drop upon his kingdom and devour
35   Incertain lookers on. What were more holy
      Than to rejoice the former queen is well?
      What holier than, for royalty's repair,
      For present comfort and for future good,
      To bless the bed of majesty again
40   With a sweet fellow to 't?

PAULINA
                              There is none worthy,
      Respecting her that's gone. Besides, the gods
      Will have fulfill'd their secret purposes;
      For has not the divine Apollo said,
45   Is 't not the tenor of his oracle,
      That King Leontes shall not have an heir
      Till his lost child be found? which that it shall,
      Is all as monstrous to our human reason
      As my Antigonus to break his grave
50   And come again to me; who, on my life,
      Did perish with the infant. 'Tis your counsel
      My lord should to the heavens be contrary,
      Oppose against their wills. *(To* LEONTES*)* Care not
            for issue;
      The crown will find an heir: great Alexander

CLEOMENES

Never say that, good lady. There are a thousand other things you could have said that would have been of greater benefit and would have made you seem kinder.

PAULINA

You are one of the people who want him to marry again.

DION

If you wouldn't have him marry again, you don't care anything for the state, or for the continuance of his royal name. Think about what dangers might befall his kingdom, and how anxious citizens might suffer, if he doesn't have a son. What is more virtuous than to rejoice that the former queen is in heaven? What would be holier than the king producing a child to restore the royal family and to make the realm safe and happy for the present and the future?

PAULINA

There is no one worthy to take the place of the queen who is gone. Besides, the gods are fulfilling their intentions. Didn't divine Apollo say, through the words of his oracle, that King Leontes should not have an heir until his lost child is found? And that seems as unlikely as the notion that my Antigonus, whom I am sure died along with the infant, will rise from his grave and return to me. Your advice is that my lord should go against the heavens and oppose their wills. (*to Leontes*) Don't worry about a son. The crown will find an heir. Great Alexander left his kingdom to the worthiest of his followers, so that his successor would be the best leader possible.

55   Left his to the worthiest; so his successor
       Was like to be the best.

LEONTES

                           Good Paulina,
       Who hast the memory of Hermione,
       I know, in honour, O, that ever I
60   Had squared me to thy counsel! then, even now,
       I might have look'd upon my queen's full eyes,
       Have taken treasure from her lips—

PAULINA

                              And left them
       More rich for what they yielded.

LEONTES

65   Thou speak'st truth.
       No more such wives; therefore, no wife: one worse,
       And better used, would make her sainted spirit
       Again possess her corpse, and on this stage,
       Where we're offenders now, appear soul-vex'd,
70   And begin, 'Why to me?'

PAULINA

                       Had she such power,
       She had just cause.

LEONTES

                 She had; and would incense me
       To murder her I married.

PAULINA

75   I should so.
       Were I the ghost that walk'd, I'd bid you mark
       Her eye, and tell me for what dull part in 't
       You chose her; then I'd shriek, that even your ears
       Should rift to hear me; and the words that follow'd
80   Should be 'Remember mine.'

LEONTES

                       Stars, stars,
       And all eyes else dead coals! Fear thou no wife;
       I'll have no wife, Paulina.

LEONTES

> Good Paulina, I know you honor the memory of
> Hermione. I wish that I had listened to you! Then I
> would now be able to look into my queen's eyes and kiss
> her treasured lips—

PAULINA

> And been the richer for having done so.

LEONTES

> You speak the truth. No wife such as that exists, so there
> will be no wife. For me to take a wife less perfect, and
> to treat her better, would make Hermione's ghost arise
> again, and she'd appear here to me and say, "Why insult
> me like this?"

PAULINA

> If she were able to, she'd be justified.

LEONTES

> She would be, and she'd drive me to murder the woman
> I married in her place.

PAULINA

> I should think so. If I were Hermione's ghost, I'd tell
> you to look at that new woman's eyes and tell me what
> about their dullness attracted you. Then I'd shriek,
> and your ears would hurt to hear me. And then I'd say,
> "Remember my eyes."

LEONTES

> They were like stars, and next to them all other eyes
> look like dead coals! Don't fear, Paulina, I won't take
> another wife.

PAULINA

Will you swear

85   Never to marry but by my free leave?

LEONTES

Never, Paulina; so be blest my spirit!

PAULINA

Then, good my lords, bear witness to his oath.

CLEOMENES

You tempt him over-much.

PAULINA

Unless another,

90   As like Hermione as is her picture,

Affront his eye—

CLEOMENES

Good madam,—

PAULINA

I have done.

Yet, if my lord will marry,—if you will, sir,

95   No remedy, but you will,—give me the office

To choose you a queen: she shall not be so young

As was your former; but she shall be such

As, walk'd your first queen's ghost, it should take joy

To see her in your arms.

LEONTES

100   My true Paulina,

We shall not marry till thou bid'st us.

PAULINA

That

Shall be when your first queen's again in breath;

Never till then.

Enter a **GENTLEMAN**

GENTLEMAN

105   One that gives out himself Prince Florizel,

Son of Polixenes, with his princess, she

The fairest I have yet beheld, desires access

To your high presence.

PAULINA

> Will you swear to never marry unless I give you
> my permission?

LEONTES

> Never, Paulina, on my life!

PAULINA

> Then, my good lords, witness his oath.

CLEOMENES

> You test him too much.

PAULINA

> Unless he sees another woman who looks as much like
> Hermione as her picture—

CLEOMENES

> Good madam—

PAULINA

> I'm done. Yet, if my lord decides to marry despite
> everything, let me choose your queen. She won't be as
> young as your former wife, but she'll be someone who
> even your first queen would rejoice to see in your arms.

LEONTES

> My faithful Paulina, I won't marry until you tell me to.

PAULINA

> That will be when your first queen is alive again, not
> until then.

A GENTLEMAN *enters.*

GENTLEMAN

> A man who calls himself Prince Florizel, son of
> Polixenes, asks to see you. With him is his princess, who
> is the fairest lady I have ever seen.

LEONTES

What with him? he comes not
110 Like to his father's greatness: his approach,
So out of circumstance and sudden, tells us
'Tis not a visitation framed, but forced
By need and accident. What train?

GENTLEMAN

But few,
115 And those but mean.

LEONTES

His princess, say you, with him?

GENTLEMAN

Ay, the most peerless piece of earth, I think,
That e'er the sun shone bright on.

PAULINA

O Hermione,
120 As every present time doth boast itself
Above a better gone, so must thy grave
Give way to what's seen now! Sir, you yourself
Have said and writ so, but your writing now
Is colder than that theme, 'She had not been,
125 Nor was not to be equall'd;'—thus your verse
Flow'd with her beauty once: 'tis shrewdly ebb'd,
To say you have seen a better.

GENTLEMAN

Pardon, madam:
The one I have almost forgot,—your pardon,—
130 The other, when she has obtain'd your eye,
Will have your tongue too. This is a creature,
Would she begin a sect, might quench the zeal
Of all professors else, make proselytes
Of who she but bid follow.

PAULINA

How! not women?

LEONTES

What is this? He arrives without the ceremony someone of his station requires. That he appears so suddenly and unexpectedly tells me that it wasn't a planned visit, but one forced by circumstances. How many does he have with him?

GENTLEMAN

Only a few, and those of rather low rank.

LEONTES

You say his princess is with him?

GENTLEMAN

Yes, and she is the most incomparable woman that the sun has ever shone upon.

PAULINA

Oh, Hermione, just as every era thinks it's better than the one past, so must you make way for a new woman. Sir, you yourself have said and written that she was never, and never would be, equaled in beauty, but now you change your mind. Your poetry was once filled with reports of her beauty, but it must have declined since you say that you have seen someone more beautiful.

GENTLEMAN

Pardon, madam. I'm sorry to say I've almost forgotten Hermione. When you see this other woman, you'll be speechless, too. If she started her own religion, it would put an end to the zeal of any other and make followers of anyone she called.

PAULINA

What? Not women, though?

GENTLEMAN

    Women will love her, that she is a woman
    More worth than any man; men, that she is
    The rarest of all women.

LEONTES

                Go, Cleomenes;
140   Yourself, assisted with your honour'd friends,
    Bring them to our embracement.

                Exeunt CLEOMENES *and others*

                Still, 'tis strange
    He thus should steal upon us.

PAULINA

                Had our prince,
145   Jewel of children, seen this hour, he had pair'd
    Well with this lord: there was not full a month
    Between their births.

LEONTES

                Prithee, no more; cease; thou know'st
    He dies to me again when talk'd of: sure,
150   When I shall see this gentleman, thy speeches
    Will bring me to consider that which may
    Unfurnish me of reason. They are come.

    Re-enter CLEOMENES *and others, with* FLORIZEL *and* PERDITA

    Your mother was most true to wedlock, prince;
    For she did print your royal father off,
155   Conceiving you: were I but twenty-one,
    Your father's image is so hit in you,
    His very air, that I should call you brother,
    As I did him, and speak of something wildly
    By us perform'd before. Most dearly welcome!
160   And your fair princess,—goddess!—O, alas!
    I lost a couple, that 'twixt heaven and earth
    Might thus have stood begetting wonder as

GENTLEMAN

> Women will love her because she is a woman more worthy than any man. Men will love her because she is the most exceptional of women.

LEONTES

> Go, Cleomenes. With the help of your friends, bring them back here for my welcome.

> > *CLEOMENES and others exit.*

> Still, it is strange that he comes to us so suddenly.

PAULINA

> If your prince, the most prized of children, were alive to see this, he would have gotten along well with this lord. They were born less than a month apart.

LEONTES

> Please, no more. Stop. You know it's like he dies again for me when you talk about him. When I see this gentleman, your words will make me think of that which makes me go mad. They are here.

> *CLEOMENES and others enter, accompanied by FLORIZEL and PERDITA.*

> Your mother was a faithful wife, prince, because in bearing you she has produced a copy of your royal father. You look and act so much like your father that if I were twenty-one, I'd call you brother just like I called him, and speak of some wild escapade we'd gotten into. You are very welcome here, and your fair princess, like a goddess! Oh, alas, I've lost two who might have stood there, too, in wonderment, as you do. And then through my own folly I lost the company and friendship of your brave father, whom I wish I could see once more in this lifetime, even if it caused me sadness.

You, gracious couple, do: and then I lost—
All mine own folly—the society,
165   Amity too, of your brave father, whom,
Though bearing misery, I desire my life
Once more to look on him.

FLORIZEL

By his command
Have I here touch'd Sicilia and from him
170   Give you all greetings that a king, at friend,
Can send his brother: and, but infirmity
Which waits upon worn times hath something seized
His wish'd ability, he had himself
The lands and waters 'twixt your throne and his
175   Measured to look upon you; whom he loves—
He bade me say so—more than all the sceptres
And those that bear them living.

LEONTES

O my brother,
Good gentleman! the wrongs I have done thee stir
180   Afresh within me, and these thy offices,
So rarely kind, are as interpreters
Of my behind-hand slackness. Welcome hither,
As is the spring to the earth. And hath he too
Exposed this paragon to the fearful usage,
185   At least ungentle, of the dreadful Neptune,
To greet a man not worth her pains, much less
The adventure of her person?

FLORIZEL

Good my lord,
She came from Libya.

LEONTES

190   Where the warlike Smalus,
That noble honour'd lord, is fear'd and loved?

FLORIZEL

Most royal sir, from thence; from him, whose daughter
His tears proclaim'd his, parting with her: thence,

FLORIZEL

> I've come to Sicilia at his command, and I bring from
> him all the greetings that a king and a friend can send
> to his brother. If it weren't for the infirmity of age that
> somewhat hinders him, he would travel here himself to
> greet you. He told me to tell you that he loves you, more
> than all the other kings alive.

LEONTES

> Oh, my brother, good gentleman! I feel the wrongs
> I've done to him all over again. And your exceptional
> kindness shows me how slow I've been in greeting you.
> You are as welcome here as the spring is to the Earth.
> And has he sent this most lovely woman here, too, across
> the dangerous and rough sea, to greet an unworthy man?

FLORIZEL

> My lord, she came from Libya.

LEONTES

> Where the fierce Smalus, that honorable lord, is both
> feared and loved?

FLORIZEL

> Most royal sir, from there, and from her father, who cried
> at her departure. From there, with a good south wind,

A prosperous south-wind friendly, we have cross'd,
195   To execute the charge my father gave me
For visiting your highness: my best train
I have from your Sicilian shores dismiss'd;
Who for Bohemia bend, to signify
Not only my success in Libya, sir,
200   But my arrival and my wife's in safety
Here where we are.

LEONTES

The blessed gods
Purge all infection from our air whilst you
Do climate here! You have a holy father,
205   A graceful gentleman; against whose person,
So sacred as it is, I have done sin:
For which the heavens, taking angry note,
Have left me issueless; and your father's blest,
As he from heaven merits it, with you
210   Worthy his goodness. What might I have been,
Might I a son and daughter now have look'd on,
Such goodly things as you!

Enter a **LORD**

LORD

Most noble sir,
That which I shall report will bear no credit,
215   Were not the proof so nigh. Please you, great sir,
Bohemia greets you from himself by me;
Desires you to attach his son, who has—
His dignity and duty both cast off—
Fled from his father, from his hopes, and with
220   A shepherd's daughter.

LEONTES

Where's Bohemia? speak.

LORD

Here in your city; I now came from him:
I speak amazedly; and it becomes

we have crossed the sea to carry out my father's request
to visit you. I have sent the best men of my entourage
back to Bohemia, to let my father know both that my trip
to Libya was successful and that my wife and I arrived
here safely.

LEONTES

May the gods keep the air fresh and healthy while you are
here! You have a great and graceful father, against whom
I have committed a sin. In return, the angry heavens have
left me childless, while your father is blessed by Heaven
with you, as he deserves. What might my life have been
like if I had a son and daughter as lovely as you two to
look at!

A **LORD** *enters.*

LORD

Most noble sir, if I didn't have such firm proof you
wouldn't believe what I'm about to tell you. Sir,
Polixenes himself greets you through me. He asks you
to hold his son, who has abandoned his royal status and
responsibilities, and who has fled from his father and his
hope of the throne with a shepherd's daughter.

LEONTES

Where is Polixenes? Tell me.

LORD

Here in your city. I just came from him. I'm astonished,
as suits my message. It seems that while he was hurrying

My marvel and my message. To your court
225 Whiles he was hastening, in the chase, it seems,
Of this fair couple, meets he on the way
The father of this seeming lady and
Her brother, having both their country quitted
With this young prince.

FLORIZEL

230   Camillo has betray'd me;
Whose honour and whose honesty till now
Endured all weathers.

LORD

                              Lay 't so to his charge:
He's with the king your father.

LEONTES

235   Who? Camillo?

LORD

Camillo, sir; I spake with him; who now
Has these poor men in question. Never saw I
Wretches so quake: they kneel, they kiss the earth;
Forswear themselves as often as they speak:
240 Bohemia stops his ears, and threatens them
With divers deaths in death.

PERDITA

                                    O my poor father!
The heaven sets spies upon us, will not have
Our contract celebrated.

LEONTES

245   You are married?

FLORIZEL

We are not, sir, nor are we like to be;
The stars, I see, will kiss the valleys first:
The odds for high and low's alike.

LEONTES

                                    My lord,
250 Is this the daughter of a king?

here to your court in pursuit of this fair couple, he met
the father and brother of the lady, who had both left their
country with the prince.

FLORIZEL

Camillo has betrayed me, though his honor and honesty
had been steadfast until now.

LORD

You may charge him with that yourself. He's with the
king, your father.

LEONTES

Who? Camillo?

LORD

Camillo, sir. I spoke with him, and he now has the poor
men in question. I've never seen anyone tremble as they
do. They kneel, and kiss the Earth, and take back what
they've said every time they speak. Polixenes refuses to
listen and threatens them with various tortures.

PERDITA

Oh, my poor father! The heavens set spies on us and
refuse to let us celebrate our vows.

LEONTES

You are married?

FLORIZEL

We aren't, sir, and it seems impossible that we will be. I
see that the stars will fall to the Earth first. Chance works
equally for the high- and the lowborn.

LEONTES

My lord, is this the daughter of a king?

FLORIZEL

She is,
When once she is my wife.

LEONTES

That 'once' I see by your good father's speed
Will come on very slowly. I am sorry,
255   Most sorry, you have broken from his liking
Where you were tied in duty, and as sorry
Your choice is not so rich in worth as beauty,
That you might well enjoy her.

FLORIZEL

Dear, look up:
260   Though Fortune, visible an enemy,
Should chase us with my father, power no jot
Hath she to change our loves. Beseech you, sir,
Remember since you owed no more to time
Than I do now: with thought of such affections,
265   Step forth mine advocate; at your request
My father will grant precious things as trifles.

LEONTES

Would he do so, I'd beg your precious mistress,
Which he counts but a trifle.

PAULINA

Sir, my liege,
270   Your eye hath too much youth in 't: not a month
'Fore your queen died, she was more worth such gazes
Than what you look on now.

LEONTES

I thought of her,
Even in these looks I made. (*to Florizel*) But your petition
275   Is yet unanswer'd. I will to your father:
Your honour not o'erthrown by your desires,
I am friend to them and you: upon which errand
I now go toward him; therefore follow me
And mark what way I make: come, good my lord.

Exeunt

FLORIZEL

> She will be, once she is my wife.

LEONTES

> I think that "once" will not be soon, given your father's speed in coming here. I am very sorry that you have gone against his wishes and your duty, and as sorry that your lady isn't as rich in rank as she is in beauty, so that you could marry her.

FLORIZEL

> Dear, cheer up. Even if Fate, which is apparently our enemy, has chased us with my father, she has no power to change our love for each other. Please, sir, remember when you were my age. Thinking of such love, come forward in my defense. If you request it, my father will grant precious things as though they were nothing.

LEONTES

> I'd beg your precious mistress's pardon if he counted her as nothing.

PAULINA

> My lord, you are too dazzled by youth. Your queen deserved those admiring glances more than this woman only a month before she died.

LEONTES

> I thought of her, even as I looked upon this woman. (*to Florizel*) But I haven't answered your request. I will tell your father that you haven't let your desire to marry this girl overwhelm your honor. I support both you and your wish. I'll go to him now on this errand. Follow me, and watch where I go. Come, my lord.

> *They exit.*

ACT 5, SCENE 2

Before LEONTES' *palace.*
Enter AUTOLYCUS *and a* GENTLEMAN

AUTOLYCUS

Beseech you, sir, were you present at this relation?

FIRST GENTLEMAN

I was by at the opening of the fardel, heard the
old shepherd deliver the manner how he found it:
whereupon, after a little amazedness, we were all
5   commanded out of the chamber; only this methought I
heard the shepherd say, he found the child.

AUTOLYCUS

I would most gladly know the issue of it.

FIRST GENTLEMAN

I make a broken delivery of the business; but the changes
I perceived in the king and Camillo were very notes of
10   admiration: they seemed almost, with staring on one
another, to tear the cases of their eyes; there was speech
in their dumbness, language in their very gesture; they
looked as they had heard of a world ransomed, or one
destroyed: a notable passion of wonder appeared in them;
15   but the wisest beholder, that knew no more but seeing,
could not say if the importance were joy or sorrow; but in
the extremity of the one, it must needs be.

Enter another GENTLEMAN

Here comes a gentleman that haply knows more.
The news, Rogero?

SECOND GENTLEMAN

20   Nothing but bonfires: the oracle is fulfilled; the king's
daughter is found: such a deal of wonder is broken out
within this hour that ballad-makers cannot be able to
express it.

ACT 5, SCENE 2

In front of LEONTES's *palace.*
AUTOLYCUS *and a* GENTLEMAN *enter.*

AUTOLYCUS

Please, sir, were you there when it was revealed?

FIRST GENTLEMAN

I was there when the bundle was opened, and heard
the old shepherd tell how he found it. Then, after some
shock, we were all told to leave the room. But as I went, I
thought I heard the shepherd say he had found the child.

AUTOLYCUS

I would love to know the result of it.

FIRST GENTLEMAN

I could only hear bits and pieces of the conversation.
But I could hear the king and Camillo speaking in tones
of admiration. They looked at each other so intently
and with such astonishment that it seemed as if their
eyes might pop out. Even their inability to speak
communicated something, and so did their gestures.
They looked as if the world had been taken hostage, or
destroyed. They were obviously amazed. But even the
most astute observer would be unable to say if it was joy
or sorrow they felt, though obviously a great deal of one
or the other.

A second GENTLEMAN *enters.*

Here comes a gentleman who perhaps knows more.
Any news, Rogero?

SECOND GENTLEMAN

Only of celebration. The oracle is fulfilled. The
king's daughter is found. So many amazing things
have happened this hour that **ballad-makers won't
be able to express them**.

*Ballads were
often composed
about sensational
events.*

Enter a third GENTLEMAN

Here comes the Lady Paulina's steward: he can deliver
25 you more. How goes it now, sir? this news which is called
true is so like an old tale, that the verity of it is in strong
suspicion: has the king found his heir?

THIRD GENTLEMAN

Most true, if ever truth were pregnant by circumstance:
that which you hear you'll swear you see, there is such
30 unity in the proofs. The mantle of Queen Hermione's,
her jewel about the neck of it, the letters of Antigonus
found with it which they know to be his character, the
majesty of the creature in resemblance of the mother,
the affection of nobleness which nature shows above her
35 breeding, and many other evidences proclaim her with
all certainty to be the king's daughter. Did you see the
meeting of the two kings?

SECOND GENTLEMAN

No.

THIRD GENTLEMAN

Then have you lost a sight, which was to be seen, cannot
40 be spoken of. There might you have beheld one joy crown
another, so and in such manner that it seemed sorrow
wept to take leave of them, for their joy waded in tears.
There was casting up of eyes, holding up of hands, with
countenances of such distraction that they were to be
45 known by garment, not by favour. Our king, being ready
to leap out of himself for joy of his found daughter, as if
that joy were now become a loss, cries 'O, thy mother, thy
mother!' then asks Bohemia forgiveness; then embraces
his son-in-law; then again worries he his daughter with
50 clipping her; now he thanks the old shepherd, which
stands by like a weather-bitten conduit of many kings'
reigns. I never heard of such another encounter, which
lames report to follow it and undoes description to do it.

A third GENTLEMAN *enters.*

Here comes Lady Paulina's servant. He can tell you more. What's happening now? This true story seems so much like a fable that it's hard to believe. Has the king found his heir?

THIRD GENTLEMAN

It's very true, if truth was ever proven by evidence. All the stories match up and are consistent. It all shows that Perdita is certainly the king's daughter— the cloak of Queen Hermione, the jewel that was found around her neck, letters in Antigonus's handwriting found with her, how much she looks like her mother, her noble bearing, which shows her to be more than a shepherd's daughter, and many other things. Did you see the meeting of the two kings?

SECOND GENTLEMAN

No.

THIRD GENTLEMAN

Then you've missed something indescribable. You would have seen one joy upon another. It was so emotional that they both wept. They raised their eyes to Heaven, clasped hands, and their faces were so contorted with emotion that you could only recognize them by their clothing. Our king, overcome with joy at having found his daughter, cried out, "Oh, your mother, your mother," as if that joy had become a loss. Then he asked Polixenes for forgiveness, then embraced his son-in-law, and then harassed his daughter with embraces. Then he thanks the old shepherd, who stands there weeping like a stone statue. I've never heard of such an event. It's impossible to tell what happened, or to describe it.

SECOND GENTLEMAN

What, pray you, became of Antigonus, that carried hence
55   the child?

THIRD GENTLEMAN

Like an old tale still, which will have matter to rehearse,
though credit be asleep and not an ear open. He was torn
to pieces with a bear: this avouches the shepherd's son;
who has not only his innocence, which seems much,
60   to justify him, but a handkerchief and rings of his that
Paulina knows.

FIRST GENTLEMAN

What became of his bark and his followers?

THIRD GENTLEMAN

Wrecked the same instant of their master's death and
in the view of the shepherd: so that all the instruments
65   which aided to expose the child were even then lost when
it was found. But O, the noble combat that 'twixt joy and
sorrow was fought in Paulina! She had one eye declined
for the loss of her husband, another elevated that the
oracle was fulfilled: she lifted the princess from the earth,
70   and so locks her in embracing, as if she would pin her to
her heart that she might no more be in danger of losing.

FIRST GENTLEMAN

The dignity of this act was worth the audience of kings
and princes; for by such was it acted.

THIRD GENTLEMAN

One of the prettiest touches of all and that which angled
75   for mine eyes, caught the water though not the fish,
was when, at the relation of the queen's death, with
the manner how she came to 't bravely confessed and
lamented by the king, how attentiveness wounded his
daughter; till, from one sign of dolour to another, she
80   did, with an 'Alas,' I would fain say, bleed tears, for I am
sure my heart wept blood. Who was most marble there
changed colour; some swooned, all sorrowed: if all the
world could have seen 't, the woe had been universal.

SECOND GENTLEMAN

> What became of Antigonus, who carried away the child?

THIRD GENTLEMAN

> That itself is like an old story, which will take effort to recount and is hard to believe. He was torn to pieces by a bear. The shepherd's son swears so, and not only does he seem innocent enough to be believed, but he also has a handkerchief and rings that Paulina recognized as belonging to Antigonus.

FIRST GENTLEMAN

> What happened to his ship and his companions?

THIRD GENTLEMAN

> They were wrecked at the same time their master was killed. The shepherd saw it happen. So all those who helped exile the child were lost. Paulina was caught between joy and sorrow! She was saddened at the loss of her husband but elated that the oracle was fulfilled. She lifted the princess in a hug, as if she could pin her to her heart so as never to lose her again.

FIRST GENTLEMAN

> This is a scene worthy of an audience of kings and princes, who were also the actors in it.

THIRD GENTLEMAN

> One of the most moving things of all, which brought me to tears, was when the king bravely and sadly told his daughter how the queen died. How intently Perdita listened! She went from sorrow to sorrow, and finally said "Alas," and seemed to bleed tears. I would say my heart nearly broke. Even the most hardened onlooker was affected. Some fainted, and all mourned. If the world could have seen it, everyone would have felt sorrow.

FIRST GENTLEMAN

Are they returned to the court?

THIRD GENTLEMAN

85   No: the princess hearing of her mother's statue, which is
in the keeping of Paulina,—a piece many years in doing
and now newly performed by that rare Italian master,
Julio Romano, who, had he himself eternity and could
put breath into his work, would beguile Nature of her
90   custom, so perfectly he is her ape: he so near to Hermione
hath done Hermione that they say one would speak to her
and stand in hope of answer: thither with all greediness of
affection are they gone, and there they intend to sup.

SECOND GENTLEMAN

I thought she had some great matter there in hand; for
95   she hath privately twice or thrice a day, ever since the
death of Hermione, visited that removed house. Shall we
thither and with our company piece the rejoicing?

FIRST GENTLEMAN

Who would be thence that has the benefit of access? every
wink of an eye some new grace will be born: our absence
100   makes us unthrifty to our knowledge. Let's along.

Exeunt GENTLEMEN

AUTOLYCUS

Now, had I not the dash of my former life in me, would
preferment drop on my head. I brought the old man and
his son aboard the prince: told him I heard them talk of a
fardel and I know not what: but he at that time, overfond
105   of the shepherd's daughter, so he then took her to be,
who began to be much sea-sick, and himself little better,
extremity of weather continuing, this mystery remained
undiscovered. But 'tis all one to me; for had I been the
finder out of this secret, it would not have relished among
110   my other discredits.

Enter SHEPHERD *and* CLOWN

FIRST GENTLEMAN

Have they returned to the court?

THIRD GENTLEMAN

No. The princess heard that Paulina keeps a statue of her mother that was made over many years and just recently finished. It was done by that Italian master, Julio Romano, who makes his subjects so close to life that, if he could breathe life into his statues, he would replace Nature. He has replicated Hermione so closely that they say that you might speak to her and expect an answer. They've gone to see it, and they intend to dine there.

SECOND GENTLEMAN

I thought Paulina had some important business there. Ever since Hermione died, she has visited that remote place privately two or three times a day. Shall we go there and join the celebration?

FIRST GENTLEMAN

Who wouldn't go who has access? Every moment you look will show a new wonder. Our absence will make us poorer in knowledge. Let's go.

The GENTLEMEN *exit.*

AUTOLYCUS

Now, if I didn't have a trace of my former life in me, the king would favor me. I brought the old man and his son aboard with the prince, and told him I heard them talk about a bundle and so on. But he was distracted by his fondness for the shepherd's daughter, who he still thought her to be at the time, and with the bad weather they both began to suffer from sea-sickness. The mystery remained undiscovered. But it's all the same to me. If I had revealed this secret, it wouldn't have gone well with my other misdeeds.

The SHEPHERD *and* YOKEL *enter, dressed as gentlemen.*

Here come those I have done good to against my will, and
already appearing in the blossoms of their fortune.

SHEPHERD

Come, boy; I am past more children, but thy sons and
daughters will be all gentlemen born.

CLOWN

115 You are well met, sir. You denied to fight with me this
other day, because I was no gentleman born. See you
these clothes? say you see them not and think me still no
gentleman born: you were best say these robes are not
gentlemen born: give me the lie, do, and try whether I am
120 not now a gentleman born.

AUTOLYCUS

I know you are now, sir, a gentleman born.

CLOWN

Ay, and have been so any time these four hours.

SHEPHERD

And so have I, boy.

CLOWN

So you have: but I was a gentleman born before my
125 father; for the king's son took me by the hand, and called
me brother; and then the two kings called my father
brother; and then the prince my brother and the princess
my sister called my father father; and so we wept, and
there was the first gentleman-like tears that ever we shed.

SHEPHERD

130 We may live, son, to shed many more.

CLOWN

Ay; or else 'twere hard luck, being in so preposterous
estate as we are.

AUTOLYCUS

I humbly beseech you, sir, to pardon me all the faults
I have committed to your worship and to give me your
135 good report to the prince my master.

Here come those men I have helped against my will, and they already are enjoying their good fortune.

SHEPHERD

Come, my boy. I won't have any more children, but your sons and daughters will be the children of a gentleman.

YOKEL

(*to Autolycus*) Good to see you, sir. You refused to fight me the other day because I wasn't a gentleman's son. Do you see these clothes? Tell me you don't see them and still think I'm not a gentleman's son. You'd be better off saying these clothes aren't from a gentleman. Lie to me, and see whether I'm not a gentleman's son.

AUTOLYCUS

Now I know you are a gentleman, sir.

YOKEL

Yes, and have been so for these past four hours.

SHEPHERD

And I've been, too, boy.

YOKEL

You have. But I became a gentleman before my father, because the king's son took me by the hand and called me "brother." Then the two kings called my father "brother." And then my brother the prince, and my sister the princess called my father "father." And so we all wept, and those were the first tears we shed as gentlemen.

SHEPHERD

May we live to shed many more, son.

YOKEL

Yes, or it would be tough luck, being in such **preposterous state** as we are.

The Yokel confuses preposterous with prosperous, thus inadvertently mocking his rise in social rank.

AUTOLYCUS

I humbly beg you, sir, to forgive me for all the ways I have offended you, and to speak well of me to the prince, my master.

SHEPHERD

Prithee, son, do; for we must be gentle, now we
are gentlemen.

CLOWN

Thou wilt amend thy life?

AUTOLYCUS

Ay, an it like your good worship.

CLOWN

140   Give me thy hand: I will swear to the prince thou art as
honest a true fellow as any is in Bohemia.

SHEPHERD

You may say it, but not swear it.

CLOWN

Not swear it, now I am a gentleman? Let boors and
franklins say it, I'll swear it.

SHEPHERD

145   How if it be false, son?

CLOWN

If it be ne'er so false, a true gentleman may swear it in the
behalf of his friend: and I'll swear to the prince thou art a
tall fellow of thy hands and that thou wilt not be drunk;
but I know thou art no tall fellow of thy hands and that
150   thou wilt be drunk: but I'll swear it, and I would thou
wouldst be a tall fellow of thy hands.

AUTOLYCUS

I will prove so, sir, to my power.

CLOWN

Ay, by any means prove a tall fellow: if I do not wonder
how thou darest venture to be drunk, not being a tall
155   fellow, trust me not. Hark! the kings and the princes,
our kindred, are going to see the queen's picture. Come,
follow us: we'll be thy good masters.

Exeunt

SHEPHERD

Yes, son, do so. We have to be gentle, now that we are gentlemen.

YOKEL

You'll reform yourself?

AUTOLYCUS

Yes, as it pleases you.

YOKEL

Give me your hand. I will swear to the prince that you are as honest as any man in Bohemia.

SHEPHERD

You may say it, but don't swear it.

YOKEL

Don't swear it, now that I am a gentleman? Let peasants and farmers simply say it. I'll swear it.

SHEPHERD

What if it turns out to be untrue, son?

YOKEL

Even if it's untrue, a true gentleman will swear it on behalf of his friend. (*to Autolycus*) And I'll swear to the prince that you are a brave man of action and that you won't be drunk. I know you aren't a brave man of action and that you will be drunk. But I'll swear it, and I hope you'll be a brave man of action.

AUTOLYCUS

I'll do my best to prove so, sir.

YOKEL

Yes, prove yourself a brave fellow. If I'm not amazed how you dare to be drunk, not being a brave man myself, don't trust me. (*noise off-stage*) Look! The kings and the princess, our family, are going to see the queen's statue. Come, follow us. We'll be your kind masters.

They exit.

ACT 5, SCENE 3

A chapel in PAULINA's *house.*
Enter LEONTES, POLIXENES, FLORIZEL, PERDITA, CAMILLO,
PAULINA, *Lords, and Attendants*

LEONTES
   O grave and good Paulina, the great comfort
   That I have had of thee!

PAULINA
         What, sovereign sir,
   I did not well I meant well. All my services
5   You have paid home: but that you have vouchsafed,
   With your crown'd brother and these your contracted
   Heirs of your kingdoms, my poor house to visit,
   It is a surplus of your grace, which never
   My life may last to answer.

LEONTES
10   O Paulina,
   We honour you with trouble: but we came
   To see the statue of our queen: your gallery
   Have we pass'd through, not without much content
   In many singularities; but we saw not
15   That which my daughter came to look upon,
   The statue of her mother.

PAULINA
        As she lived peerless,
   So her dead likeness, I do well believe,
   Excels whatever yet you look'd upon
20   Or hand of man hath done; therefore I keep it
   Lonely, apart. But here it is: prepare
   To see the life as lively mock'd as ever
   Still sleep mock'd death: behold, and say 'tis well.

   PAULINA *draws a curtain and discovers* HERMIONE *standing*
   like a statue

ACT 5, SCENE 3

A chapel in PAULINA'S *house.*

LEONTES, POLIXENES, FLORIZEL, PERDITA, CAMILLO, *and*
PAULINA *enter, along with Lords and Attendants.*

LEONTES

> Oh, serious and good Paulina, you have given me
> great comfort.

PAULINA

> Sir, even if I didn't always succeed in doing well, I always
> meant well. You've repaid all my services. The fact that
> you've vowed to visit my poor house with your royal
> brother and the heirs of each of your kingdoms shows
> your immense grace, which I'll never be able to repay.

LEONTES

> Oh, Paulina, we honor you by disturbing you. But
> we came to see the statue of my queen. We've passed
> through your gallery, which has many amazing items, but
> we didn't see what my daughter came to see: the statue of
> her mother.

PAULINA

> Just as she was without peer in life, I believe that her dead
> statue is more beautiful that anything you've seen or that
> man has created. So I keep it apart from the others. But
> here it is. Prepare to see life mimicked as well as sleep
> mimics death. Look, and say it is beautiful.

> PAULINA *draws a curtain to reveal* HERMIONE, *standing like a
> statue.*

I like your silence, it the more shows off
25   Your wonder: but yet speak; first, you, my liege,
Comes it not something near?

LEONTES

                        Her natural posture!
Chide me, dear stone, that I may say indeed
Thou art Hermione; or rather, thou art she
30   In thy not chiding, for she was as tender
As infancy and grace. But yet, Paulina,
Hermione was not so much wrinkled, nothing
So aged as this seems.

POLIXENES

                O, not by much.

PAULINA

35   So much the more our carver's excellence;
Which lets go by some sixteen years and makes her
As she lived now.

LEONTES

             As now she might have done,
So much to my good comfort, as it is
40   Now piercing to my soul. O, thus she stood,
Even with such life of majesty, warm life,
As now it coldly stands, when first I woo'd her!
I am ashamed: does not the stone rebuke me
For being more stone than it? O royal piece,
45   There's magic in thy majesty, which has
My evils conjured to remembrance and
From thy admiring daughter took the spirits,
Standing like stone with thee.

PERDITA

                    And give me leave,
50   And do not say 'tis superstition, that
I kneel and then implore her blessing. Lady,
Dear queen, that ended when I but began,
Give me that hand of yours to kiss.

I like your silence. It shows how awed you are. But you, my lord, answer first—doesn't it look like her?

LEONTES

Just as she stood! Reprimand me, dear stone, that I say that you are indeed Hermione. Or rather, don't reprimand me, since you are so like her and she had a tender nature. But still, Paulina, Hermione wasn't this wrinkled and not as old as this statue appears.

POLIXENES

Oh, not at all.

PAULINA

That shows how excellent the sculptor is. He thinks about what she would look like now, sixteen years having passed, and makes her look as though she lived now.

LEONTES

This statue comforts me now, as she might have done, as much as it pains me to look at it. Oh, when I first courted her she stood just this way, with as much majesty and warmth as this stone has coldness. I am ashamed. Doesn't the stone chastise me for being colder than it is? Oh, royal piece of art, there's magic in your regal appearance, which has brought all my foul deeds to mind and has made your admiring daughter stand as still as stone like you.

PERDITA

Let me kneel and implore her blessing, and don't say it is superstition. Lady, dear queen, who died just as I was beginning to live, give me your hand to kiss.

PAULINA

O, patience!
55   The statue is but newly fix'd, the colour's not dry.

CAMILLO

My lord, your sorrow was too sore laid on,
Which sixteen winters cannot blow away,
So many summers dry; scarce any joy
Did ever so long live; no sorrow
60   But kill'd itself much sooner.

POLIXENES

Dear my brother,
Let him that was the cause of this have power
To take off so much grief from you as he
Will piece up in himself.

PAULINA

65   Indeed, my lord,
If I had thought the sight of my poor image
Would thus have wrought you,—for the stone is mine—
I'd not have show'd it.

LEONTES

Do not draw the curtain.

PAULINA

70   No longer shall you gaze on 't, lest your fancy
May think anon it moves.

LEONTES

Let be, let be.
Would I were dead, but that, methinks, already—
What was he that did make it? See, my lord,
75   Would you not deem it breathed? and that those veins
Did verily bear blood?

POLIXENES

Masterly done:
The very life seems warm upon her lip.

LEONTES

The fixture of her eye has motion in 't,
80   As we are mock'd with art.

PAULINA

Oh, wait! The statue is still new, and the paint isn't dry.

CAMILLO

My lord, your sorrow is too deep. Sixteen winters haven't blown it away, and many summers haven't dried it. No joy lives that long, and neither has any sorrow.

POLIXENES

My dear brother, since I was a cause of this situation, let me take some grief from you to make a part of myself.

PAULINA

Indeed, my lord, if I had thought seeing this poor statue would have made you so distraught, I wouldn't have shown it to you. (*she moves to close the curtain*)

LEONTES

Don't draw the curtain.

PAULINA

Don't look at it any longer, or you'll imagine soon that it moves.

LEONTES

Let it be. If only I were dead, but I think already—Who made it? Look, my lord, wouldn't you say it took a breath? And that those veins were filled with blood?

POLIXENES

It's masterfully done. Her mouth seems warmed with breath.

LEONTES

Her eyes seem to move, as though we are mocked by art.

PAULINA

I'll draw the curtain:
My lord's almost so far transported that
He'll think anon it lives.

LEONTES

O sweet Paulina,
85   Make me to think so twenty years together!
No settled senses of the world can match
The pleasure of that madness. Let 't alone.

PAULINA

I am sorry, sir, I have thus far stirr'd you: but
I could afflict you farther.

LEONTES

90   Do, Paulina;
For this affliction has a taste as sweet
As any cordial comfort. Still, methinks,
There is an air comes from her: what fine chisel
Could ever yet cut breath? Let no man mock me,
95   For I will kiss her.

PAULINA

Good my lord, forbear:
The ruddiness upon her lip is wet;
You'll mar it if you kiss it, stain your own
With oily painting. Shall I draw the curtain?

LEONTES

100   No, not these twenty years.

PERDITA

So long could I
Stand by, a looker on.

PAULINA

Either forbear,
Quit presently the chapel, or resolve you
105   For more amazement. If you can behold it,
I'll make the statue move indeed, descend
And take you by the hand; but then you'll think—
Which I protest against—I am assisted
By wicked powers.

PAULINA

> I'll draw the curtain. My lord is so overwhelmed that soon he'll think it lives.

LEONTES

> Oh, sweet Paulina, make me think so for twenty more years! No sanity would match the pleasure of that madness. Leave it alone.

PAULINA

> I'm sorry, sir, that I've made you so agitated, but to leave it would make it worse.

LEONTES

> Do leave it, Paulina. This agitation is as sweet as any revitalizing comfort. Still, I think air is coming from her. What amazing artist could cut breath from stone? Don't let anyone make fun of me, but I will kiss her.

PAULINA

> Don't do it, my lord. The red of her lips is wet. You'll ruin it if you kiss it, and you'll get your own lips covered in oil paint. Shall I draw the curtain?

LEONTES

> No, not for twenty years.

PERDITA

> I could stand here that long, looking at her.

PAULINA

> Either resist the temptation and leave the chapel, or prepare yourselves for more amazement. If you can take it, I'll make the statue move, step down from her pedestal, and take you by the hand. But then you'll think I'm a witch, though I swear I am not.

LEONTES

110   What you can make her do,
      I am content to look on: what to speak,
      I am content to hear; for 'tis as easy
      To make her speak as move.

PAULINA

                       It is required
115   You do awake your faith. Then all stand still;
      On: those that think it is unlawful business
      I am about, let them depart.

LEONTES

                    Proceed:
      No foot shall stir.

PAULINA

120   Music, awake her; strike!

                                           Music

      'Tis time; descend; be stone no more; approach;
      Strike all that look upon with marvel. Come,
      I'll fill your grave up: stir, nay, come away,
      Bequeath to death your numbness, for from him
125   Dear life redeems you. You perceive she stirs:

HERMIONE *comes down*

      Start not; her actions shall be holy as
      You hear my spell is lawful: do not shun her
      Until you see her die again; for then
      You kill her double. Nay, present your hand:
130   When she was young you woo'd her; now in age
      Is she become the suitor?

LEONTES

                    O, she's warm!
      If this be magic, let it be an art
      Lawful as eating.

POLIXENES

135   She embraces him.

CAMILLO

> She hugs him. If she is really alive, let her speak, too.

POLIXENES

> Yes, and tell us where she has lived, or how she's come back to life.

PAULINA

> If you were told she was alive, you would consider it a fable. But it seems she is alive, even though she doesn't speak. Look for a while. (*to Perdita*) Please, intervene, fair madam. Kneel down and ask for your mother's blessing. Look, good lady—our Perdita is found.

HERMIONE

> You gods, look down and pour your blessings upon my daughter's head! Tell me, my child, where have you been kept safe? Where have you lived? How did you find yourself in your father's court? Paulina told me the oracle gave hope that you were still alive, so I stayed alive to see you someday.

PAULINA

> There's enough time for that later, and they might want you to answer the same questions. Go together, you happy people, and all rejoice. Like an old turtledove, I'll take myself off to a solitary bough and mourn my husband, who will never be found again.

LEONTES

> Oh, peace, Paulina! You should take a husband that I approve of, as I take a wife that you approve of. This

165 As I by thine a wife: this is a match,
And made between 's by vows. Thou hast found mine;
But how, is to be question'd; for I saw her,
As I thought, dead, and have in vain said many
A prayer upon her grave. I'll not seek far—
170 For him, I partly know his mind—to find thee
An honourable husband. Come, Camillo,
And take her by the hand, whose worth and honesty
Is richly noted and here justified
By us, a pair of kings. Let's from this place.
175 What! look upon my brother: both your pardons,
That e'er I put between your holy looks
My ill suspicion. This is your son-in-law,
And son unto the king, who, heavens directing,
Is troth-plight to your daughter. Good Paulina,
180 Lead us from hence, where we may leisurely
Each one demand an answer to his part
Perform'd in this wide gap of time since first
We were dissever'd: hastily lead away.

Exeunt

is a contract, vowed between us. You have found mine, though I don't know how, since I saw her and believed her to be dead, and I've futilely said several prayers on her grave. I won't have to look far to find you an honorable husband, since I know his mind already. Come, Camillo, take her by the hand. Her worth and honesty is well known and affirmed by both Polixenes and me. Let's leave this place. (*to Hermione*) Look at my brother! I beg both your pardons for having suspected sin in your innocent glances. This is your son-in-law, the son of Polixenes, who is engaged to your daughter. Good Paulina, lead us away from here, and we'll each answer for what we've all done in this wide expanse of time since we first separated. Quickly, lead us away.

They exit.